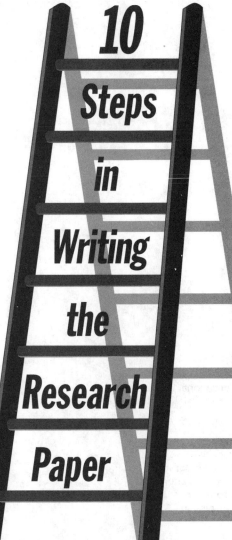

10 Steps in Writing the Research Paper

Roberta H. Markman, Ph.D., Professor
California State University,
Long Beach, California

Peter T. Markman, Professor
Fullerton College
Fullerton, California

and

Marie L. Waddell, Former Professor
The University of Texas
El Paso, Texas

Fifth Edition

All inquiries should be addressed to:
Barron's Educational Series, Inc.
250 Wireless Boulevard
Hauppauge, NY 11788

Library of Congress Catalog Card No. 94-72109

International Standard Book No. 0-8120-1868-0

PRINTED IN THE UNITED STATES OF AMERICA
4567   8800   98765432

CONTENTS

PREFACE

We are delighted that the success of this manual in meeting the needs of both the high school and college student as well as the graduate scholar now, on the thirtieth anniversary of its first printing, warrants a fifth edition. Experienced research writers have profited from the manual's suggested techniques and the numerous models for correct form; inexperienced students have felt the security of being able to follow definite steps in order to write papers with the least wasted effort, the greatest accuracy in form, and the assurance that the finished papers would meet the most exacting standards of research. The methodology outlined herein, the succinctness of its presentation, and the extensive coverage of its forms have received praise from both students and instructors throughout the country during the past thirty years.

We acknowledge the work of our late colleague Professor Emeritus Marie Waddell of the University of Texas, El Paso on the original edition of this manual. Her passing almost thirty years ago was a great loss, and although we have changed the text considerably, her encouragement and contribution continue to be an inspiration.

Although this new edition retains the compact format for which the earlier four have been praised, all the materials have been updated. It includes various changes in forms for documentation, such as the new MLA and APA style changes; new sources for basic reference; new computer resources for informational and bibliographical search processes including the use of CD-ROMs; and documented papers with a profusion of accompanying footnotes and an extensive bibliography to illustrate every conceivable form and technique for the student. In addition, the outline for the new paper is written to exemplify a comparative study with an interdisciplinary approach; it represents a new and important focus in education and a challenging area for further research. The sample paper itself is designed to develop only the thesis for the outline, but no problem of documentation is ignored.

We have each had the marvelous experience of sending our students off with this book as their only "instructor" and of receiving creative and accurately documented research in return. We therefore feel confident that this edition will do an even better job of instructing and of making the process of writing the research paper a process of ten easy steps.

HUNTINGTON HARBOUR, CALIFORNIA   *Roberta Hoffman Markman*
MARCH 1, 1994   *Peter Tollin Markman*

INTRODUCTION TO RESEARCH

Research is the disciplined process of investigating and seeking facts that will lead one to discover the truth about something. This truth, stated as one's thesis,* is a result of the facts one discovers, and it must be proved conclusively to the reader by the facts selected. The thesis may not be a statement of preconceived opinion or prejudice, nor may the paper be a stringing together of related quotations and a collection of footnotes.

The research paper, a formal presentation of these discovered facts, provides the evidence one needs to defend the opinion expressed as the thesis. Consequently, one must state how and where these facts were found. If they were discovered from what other people have said or written, the student must tell who said them and where they were said so that the reader could find them also; if they were discovered by direct observation, the student must describe this experience so that the reader could repeat it and observe the same phenomena or facts. The opinion, which is the thesis, the analysis of the material on which it is based, and the conclusions one draws from that material are the most important parts of the final paper. These are subjectively presented while the facts, which provide the supporting points, are objectively presented and carefully documented.

During the process of research, the student learns to select, evaluate, and analyze facts; to discipline habits of thought and work; and, most important, to think—to create a new angle of vision. In this sense only, the research paper is original; but it is important enough in itself to justify the work involved in its creation.

Because nothing else so clearly reveals the true quality and merit of the writer's mind, the research paper becomes a valid criterion for judging the disciplined work habits and the intellectual maturity of the student.

---

*See Research Terms Defined, pp. 133–136.

THE TEN STEPS IN RESEARCH

There is always more than one way of accomplishing any task, and doing research is no exception. After much trial and error, the experienced researcher usually arrives at some system that has proved itself to be the best for him or her. However the individual systems may vary, there are ten basic steps that provide a logical method for research. They result in an ease of procedure for the researcher, the ultimate economy of time and effort, the assurance that comes from following a time-tested procedure, accuracy in the result, and the most universal acceptance by examining scholars. As you proceed, you may think that you can eliminate a step or two in the process, only to find later that you have created some extra ones to make up for the detour. So watch your step!

Step 1   FIND A SUBJECT.

Step 2   READ A GENERAL ARTICLE.

Step 3   FORMULATE A TEMPORARY THESIS AND A TEMPORARY OUTLINE.

Step 4   PREPARE THE PRELIMINARY BIBLIOGRAPHY.

Step 5   TAKE NOTES FROM RELEVANT SOURCES.

Step 6   LABEL NOTECARDS AND REVISE THE WORKING OUTLINE.

Step 7   WRITE THE FIRST DRAFT.

Step 8   REVISE THE TEXT; WRITE AN INTRODUCTION AND A CONCLUSION.

Step 9   FILL IN PARENTHETICAL REFERENCES OR FOOTNOTES ON THE DRAFT.

Step 10   PUT THE PAPER IN FINAL FORM.

STEP

FIND A SUBJECT

Finding a topic that will interest you, one that is worth your time to investigate and one for which you will have the necessary time and materials, is an extremely important step in writing the research paper. You need not be familiar with a subject before doing research on it, but you should have some interest in the general area it involves because you will be working with that subject for a long period of time.

When the general subject is not assigned by your instructor, you can usually find one by examining your own interests, your background, or the other courses you are studying. There are other considerations that will limit the possibilities from which you may choose.

Your choice of a suitable subject for investigation will often be determined by whether or not you are interested in reading or investigating—and consequently analyzing—the original material directly and therefore working with primary sources* or whether you are interested in investigating what others have said about your subject and therefore working with secondary sources. The usual college assignment involves the latter. Your choice will be determined further when you eliminate unsuitable subjects. Some subjects are not worth investigating; they are either too trivial, merely factual, or obviously routine. Others are often too new or current for conclusive study; a research paper must be factual, not conjectural, and must therefore be based on a variety of dependable sources. The availability of resource

---

*See Research Terms Defined, pp. 133–136.

materials will vary with time and locale, so you must know your area and your library. And finally, some subjects have never been suitable for research: a biography summarized from secondary sources, the entire history of anything, or any subject that you will investigate with a closed mind.

STEP

READ A GENERAL ARTICLE

After you have decided on a subject, the next step is to read a general, authoritative article (such as one in the *Encyclopaedia Britannica* or *Americana*) or browse through a scholarly book concerned with the general subject so that you can see what the possibilities and ramifications of the subject are. You will, in this first investigation, find out whether a subject is too broad to use without strict limitation or too narrow to consider at all. You will also orient yourself and become familiar with the general area in which you will be working. This reading will not only suggest ideas about how you should begin to limit your chosen, general subject but will also suggest a number of possible theses inherent in it.

Sometimes a single sentence or phrase in this article will gain your attention and suggest a question you will want to investigate. In fact, if your chosen subject is at all interesting to you, it would be almost impossible to read any general article without finding phrases or sentences that will challenge you to investigate further some aspect of that subject. Look for ideas that prompt you to ask why or how they are true or in what specific way they may be true. These ideas will provide a basis upon which you will formulate a temporary thesis and a temporary outline (discussed in STEP 3).

If, for example, you are studying French and read a general article about France, you will find countless possibilities for research topics ranging from a comparative study of the French and American revolutions to the study of a particular influence (political, military, economic, religious) on the French character. If you are studying world literature and decide to write about Anton Chekhov (because you enjoyed seeing one of his plays), you might be alerted by any of the following statements: he contributed to the comic papers in Russia during the 1880s; he visited a convict island named Sakhalin and wrote a book about it that effected changes in the regime of that penal colony; his stories are developed along "calculated curves"; his masterpiece, *My Life*, is filled with symbols that give it an almost religious character. Such statements should arouse your curiosity, make you want to know more about some particular aspect of Chekhov's work, and send you searching for information that might substantiate any thesis you finally decide to develop. Certainly, such ideas should point out many fascinating paths for you to explore.

Any time you browse through an encyclopedia or a book, you will find wonderful surprises and delightful reading that may prove to be "an arch wherethro' gleams that untravelled world" of knowledge and understanding that awaits all students. Some subject you once thought or heard about but never had a chance to pursue may challenge you to look into its various implications. Even a cursory reading of almost any general article will certainly prove that your problem will never be one of not finding some idea to research; your only problem will be deciding which of the myriad facets of knowledge on life you will choose to investigate and then reveal in your research project. No matter what thesis suggests itself as you read an encyclopedia article or book, your pursuit of it will enable you to take a giant step toward an increased perception, awareness, and enjoyment of the all-too-often hidden world around you.

STEP

FORMULATE A TEMPORARY THESIS AND A TEMPORARY OUTLINE

After you have found a general subject and have read a general article for background, you must next decide how you will work with the topic you have chosen. You might, for example, have selected several authors as the subject of your paper. You will have access to books and articles that deal with facts about their personal lives, their work, their environment, the influences on their lives and work, and the significance of their influence on others. Certainly, there would be no value in simply restating the facts and opinions as you have read them; you could not retell them all, and you would have no criterion for deciding how to select those that you would retell. Consequently, you will have to decide to concentrate on some point that your preliminary reading has suggested is an arguable truth about your topic and that further reading would probably substantiate and clarify. Just as the creative artist is led to make a final statement of truth about some aspect of life by observing and selecting from the myriad details of life's experiences, so you, as a researcher, must be able to crystallize a statement of truth by observing and selecting significant details from the wealth of material you will find on your topic. This truth, stated in a simple sentence, provides you with a temporary thesis. It is a statement of your opinion, a conclusion that, from what you have read, you have reason to believe can be proven, but that you are scholar enough to discard or alter later if you uncover facts that prove it invalid. A good thesis is never the statement of a preconceived notion or a personal prejudice that you could prove only by distorting or ignoring facts, nor is it the statement of any indisputable fact about which further investigation would reveal nothing. It must express an idea that is arguable or debatable or one that demands further explanation. Because it is an idea, it must be expressed as a full sentence, never just a phrase. "Mythology as art" is not a thesis. "A culture often expresses its mythology both visually and verbally" is an acceptable thesis. As a thesis, it requires further explanation and research because it is not self-explanatory.

If, for example, you wanted to do your research on some area of mythology, you might find in the course of your reading that you are surprised to learn that the Greeks portrayed even their most important gods and goddesses, such as Zeus and his wife Hera, as people like themselves who, although powerful and immortal, had many human frailties. The almighty Zeus, for example, was often guilty of thievery and promiscuity, as well as trickery to hide his many infidelities from his wife. Your discovery would not, however, justify a thesis that states that most Greek myths are just stories that show how evil the major gods are. Such a thesis would be based on a preconceived notion showing the limitations of your own understanding of the complexity of the subject. Neither would you consider a thesis statement saying that many early societies developed their own mythologies about the lives of the gods because this is an indisputable fact and there is very little to argue with or prove. However, because you might have realized from reading further that each culture differs dramatically in the way it thinks about the nature of its gods, you might consider an investigation of the similarities and differences in the ways that two, or possibly even three, different cultures look at their gods or how they conceptualize the relationship of mankind to the gods they have created.

Or perhaps as a result of reading in a general article that there are many similarities between African creation myths, which tell how the world and mankind came into being, and myths concerning death and the mystery surrounding death, you might be challenged to investigate the relationship between the creation and fertility myths and myths about death in the mythology of the Korumba people of Africa.

On the other hand, you might have been alerted by a statement in a general article that explains how a particular Mexican mask is used in a ritual that "acts out" the story of a myth about the Aztec god Quet-zalcoatl. You might decide to show how the details of the myth are translated into the specific actions of a ritual. Or you might be inter-ested in finding out how and why certain rituals are practiced in some areas of Mexico and omitted from others. In other words, you will choose one aspect of what you have read and investigate it to ascer-tain its validity.

Or after attending an exhibition of ancient Egyptian art and reading the catalog from it, you might realize how valuable it would be to know something about Egyptian mythology; you might even wonder whether there is a strong relationship between the art you saw at the museum and the Egyptian myths you find in your library. That ques-tion could challenge you to formulate a thesis that involves a study of the relationship of art and mythology in ancient Egypt or in another early culture that you would like to investigate. However, you would see very quickly that, because of the innumerable perspectives from which art and mythology can be compared, there are too many possi-bilities for development in one paper. Therefore, you might scan gen-eral articles covering various aspects of Egyptian mythology as well as of Egyptian art to find out whether there is some concept common to both that could form the basis of a comparative study of the two. You might find, for example, that Egyptian creation myths are the subjects of much of the art that attempts to express visually the mythology of "the beginning." A comparative study of the two modes of expression would now give you a basis upon which to narrow and reformulate your temporary thesis.

Although the thesis that you develop now is necessarily a temporary one because you have not accumulated all the available facts yet, it does provide you with an angle of vision from which you can continue your research. You now know how you are going to focus on your sub-ject, and you are ready to formulate a temporary outline. As you search in your reading and note-taking for the answers to the chal-lenging question suggested by your thesis, you will, of course, re-eval-uate your facts and modify your first opinion until you are closer to the ultimate truth, the discovery of which is always the purpose of your research.

It is important to limit your temporary thesis as soon as possible so that, within the limits of the time in which you have to work and the projected or assigned length of the finished paper, the truth of that thesis statement can be investigated thoroughly. No factor is more often responsible for a poor research paper than is the failure to limit a thesis. It is obvious that the less area you try to cover, the more depth you can explore and the more valuable your finished paper will be. As you do your research, you will probably keep narrowing your thesis and limiting the scope of your research to express an idea that can be thoroughly and realistically handled within the space limitation of your paper.

One way to help you limit your thesis is to write a very short, preliminary temporary outline listing in sentence form the main ideas that you hope to develop in order to prove your thesis. Then look to see if any one of those points might serve as the thesis itself. Continue to go through that process until you feel you have limited your thesis as much as possible. Although this thesis is necessarily a temporary one because you have not accumulated all the available facts yet, it does provide you with an angle of vision from which you can continue your research. You now know how you are going to focus on your subject and how you are going to select the material for your research. You are ready now to formulate a more complete temporary outline.

TEMPORARY OUTLINE

The particular angle of vision of your limited thesis will automatically suggest and determine the temporary outline you need to work with. If you formulate a thesis stating that humanity's attempt to understand the basic phenomena of life is expressed symbolically both verbally in mythology and visually in art, you would be compelled to investigate the truth of that statement. You would need to (1) find out how and to what extent mythology and art are symbolically expressed, (2) discover what basic phenomena of life are expressed both visually and verbally, and (3) consider how and to what extent the visual and verbal expression are comparable in expressing the attitudes and beliefs of their respective cultures. At this point you still may not be certain that you can find a sufficient basis for comparison, but it is obvious from the outset that these three basic concerns, which constitute the points of your temporary outline, must be investigated before you can conclusively state your thesis as truth. Similarly, a logical analysis of any thesis that you choose to work with will suggest the points for your temporary outline. It is important that you state them as sentences because only a sentence can state a complete idea. Then when you put them into the temporary outline, you will know exactly the point that you are going to make. They outline the path along which you and your reader must travel before the statement you first wrote as a temporary thesis can be stated as a valid conclusion and become your final thesis. A topic outline is too ambiguous to accomplish this task.

With the formulation of your thesis as a temporary objective and with an outline statement of the points by which you can logically reach it, you have the necessary criteria by which, with a minimum of wasted effort, to select books for your bibliography (STEP 4) and to choose information for your notecards (STEP 5).

In setting up your temporary outline you are actually using a deductive process. You have temporarily accepted a general statement or premise, and you are going to investigate your sources to see whether or not that premise can be substantially supported by facts. Because a generality would be too superficial to work with unless it is supported by specific and valid evidence, it is extremely important that you use the most authoritative sources available from which to find your information. You must be wary of unsigned editorial columns or magazine articles that are not carefully documented. For this reason, also, you must consult many different sources representing a wide range of thinking in order to make your paper valuable as research. However, in spite of the fact that your temporary outline is the result of a deductive process, your final thesis and outline must be inductively developed. That is, you must eventually analyze your material or the facts accumulated and change your temporary thesis so that it ultimately states an accurate result or conclusion of the material you have observed and presented. The temporary thesis, then, is the statement of a hunch or of an educated guess; the final thesis is the result of research and is a statement of what you now believe to be true. You see it as the only conclusion to which one could come from the material that you have selected and presented. And your outline shows the means by which you arrived at your thesis so that your reader can follow the process step by step with you. *See* STEP 6 for further help in writing your outline.

STEP

PREPARE THE PRELIMINARY BIBLIOGRAPHY

WHY A PRELIMINARY BIBLIOGRAPHY IS NECESSARY

There are several reasons why, before you begin to do your research, it is important to prepare a preliminary bibliography even though it will include books you will never see or use.

1. You must be sure that adequate information on the subject is available to you and that your thesis is not hackneyed.

2. You must allow time to order any pertinent published materials that you may need to obtain through the interlibrary loan service. There is a nominal charge for postage, and you should be prepared to wait at least a week.

3. You need to become familiar with the type of research that has been done on your topic.

4. From seeing a variety of titles, you will learn how your chosen thesis might be further limited or broadened.

5. You will be given clues about titles, subjects, and authors relating to your particular subject; for example, in looking up *Mythology*, you will find a section on *Creation Myths* which would lead you to *Types of Creation Myths* or *Origins of Creation Myths* as well as *Theories of Creation Myths* and thence to the specific names of mythologists who have much to say about creation myths, such as Sir James Frazer or Joseph Campbell.

6. As you prepare your bibliography and later as you browse through the material, it is urgent that you evaluate and critically examine your sources. Certainly everything in print is not valuable. By considering some important questions you will be able to evaluate your sources with some confidence:

   a. Does the author document sources in footnotes at the bottom of the page or endnotes at the end of a chapter or book? It is important to know where the information that you are reading came from. Does the author include a bibliography? This is an indication of the author's awareness of other research that has been done in the field.

   b. What is the date of the publication you are using and of the sources the author is using? If your topic requires current information, outdated material will be of no use, and if further research has been done even on something that is not current, what you say will mean very little.

   c. Is the author an authority in the field? Often the book jacket or information at the beginning or end of an article gives the author's credentials. You might want to check in such works as the *Dictionary of American Scholars* or *American Men and Women of Science* to find out something about the author's background.

   d. Have you seen references to the author in the bibliographies of other works dealing with the same subject? Usually experts in a particular field are referred to frequently in other works.

   e. Who has published the material? A university press usually publishes scholarly, well-researched material and some of the best known publishers are usually reliable. However, a vanity press or a popular magazine would normally not be a valuable source, whereas periodicals that cater to specialists would be.

WHERE TO FIND A PRELIMINARY BIBLIOGRAPHY

There are many places where you will find a listing of materials that you can include in your preliminary bibliography. Of course, your bibliography will change considerably before it becomes final because many of the titles you find in your preliminary search will not be available, some will not be useful, and new sources will be added constantly as you read. Do not look in only one place for your sources. Try to investigate each of the following sections in the libraries available to you.*

1. Online Bibliographic Computer Search

Most libraries provide two types of online computer searches. One enables you to search among all the holdings that exist in the library via an online catalog. The other enables you to search for materials that exist elsewhere either via a personal computer and telephone communications to access remote mainframe databases that exist either in reference works such as bibliographies or indexes or via a laser disc called a CD-ROM (compact disc-read only memory).

Online searching to find the materials that exist in your school library involves the use of a personal computer. Most libraries now make it possible for students to conduct their own self-service search. Ask the librarian if you have any concerns about using the library's computer. The guidelines provided here apply to the most commonly used systems. The screen will give you command "prompts" to help you find the material. Although every library has a slightly different system, usually to get started you need to press <CLEAR> or type STA (start) and then press <RETURN>.

Other possible commands:

A= enables you to search for an item by author. After A= type the last name of the author followed by a space and the first name.

T= enables you to search for an item by title. Type the title without any initial article (such as *a, an, the*).

---

*See also The Library, pp. 128–132. See also Reference Materials and Style Manuals, pp. 138–146.

S= enables you to search for material by subject matter. You will need to type the official Library of Congress Subject Heading on your screen; ask the librarian to help you find a list of those that can be used.

C= enables you to search by call number; type in as much of the number as you know. Often using the call number of one book on the subject will lead you to others written about material in the same area.

After typing a command, always press the <RETURN> key, and then the computer will bring up the screen you are looking for. Usually it makes no difference whether you use lower- or upper-case letters. When a list of titles, subjects, authors comes on the screen, you may type in the number of the item about which you want to request more information, and then a more detailed screen will appear.

EXAMPLE OF AN ENTRY IN THE ONLINE COMPUTER CATALOG

```
BL311          C263          1986
Campbell, Joseph, 1904-1987

The inner reaches of outer space: metaphor as myth
and as religion.

PUB INFO:    Joseph Campbell.
             New York: A. van derMarck Editions,
             c1986.
DESCRIPT:    155 p. : ill. (some col.) ; 25 cm.
NOTE 1:      Includes bibliographical references and
             index.
SUBJECT 1:   Mythology.
SUBJECT 2:   Religion.
SUBJECT 3:   Metaphor—Religious aspects.
ISBN:        0912383097
LCCN:        84-40776
OCLC NO:     #13008516
```

NOTE: Computer systems vary in different libraries, so the format may be different in your library, but the information will be similar.

The second type of computer search of the abstracts and various periodical indexes that exist for finding materials in a particular area of study might involve some monetary charges. For example, BRS (Bibliographic Retrieval Services) gives you access to over 30 other databases, and Dialog contains over 100 databases that catalog a wide range of subjects, such as government, humanities, physical science, business, education, and health. This material can usually be located according to author or subject. Such a search will produce a list (or the entire article) of references, mainly to journal and newspaper articles, on the topic being researched. A new series of databases that will make all kinds of information available to facilitate your search appears every week. Be sure to ask the librarian for a list of available databases and what they contain.

A computer library search is ideal for basic research for a term paper or project. It has the great advantage of saving time, providing the most current information, and allowing for detailed subject specificity. As a result you will get a much more complete listing of references on any particular subject, and often it will help to determine the potential for pursuing a particular focus within the general parameters of a subject. The comprehensiveness of the listings will often be determined by your strategy in conducting the search, and of course, listings can probably never be 100% complete.

Doing your own search is fun, especially if you enjoy working with computers and discovering their capabilities. No specific experience is necessary because it is set up for students to do the work on their own, and there are usually librarians who are ready to help with any technical problems that might arise. The computer generates very clear step-by-step instructions on the screen as you go along, and most libraries have a manual that will help you with your search strategy and database selection. The manual usually informs you of the cost of the search, the times of day when the search is less expensive than other times, the method of signing up for a terminal to conduct such a search, and which database vendors are available through that library's system. However, if you prefer to have a librarian conduct the search for you, check to see how you can arrange to have that done and what the additional cost will be. Generally, a broader range of databases is available to librarians than to you; this could be important if your project is extensive or if you are not getting the results you expected on your own.

There are two types of databases: bibliographic and full text. The former consists of a list of bibliographic references to articles and often includes a short abstract of particular ones. The full text databases include both the references and the full text of the article.

An effective and economical search depends on your advance preparation for it:

a. The first step is to set up a "search statement" such as: "Mesoamerican rituals involve images, symbols, myths."

b. From this statement identify the main concepts or keywords that will be used in the search: "images," "symbols," "myths," "rituals," "Mesoamerica."

c. Look over the areas on the particular databases that are available to you and find those that are appropriate for your particular search.

d. Then you will use a printed database thesaurus, which has more keywords for your database, to help you describe your research needs or make up your own keywords to add to the previous ones, such as: "costumes," "mythology," "cosmology," "spirituality," "religion," "gods," "Mexico."

e. Decide how to limit or expand these concepts to get closer to what you are looking for, such as "Mexican mythology," "Mexican rituals" in a particular century or place, and so on.

You are now ready to use the computer and enter your research terms. You may simply read the material on the screen, print the results, download the results onto a floppy disk, or do all of these.

The screen will let you know how many articles the keywords you have entered will generate. If you find too many entries that are not relevant, you can limit your keywords and ask for articles that have only "Mexican and mythology" involved or "symbols and rituals in Mexico." If you find that there will be too few entries, you can expand the possibilities by asking for "masks or rituals or mythology in Mexico."

CD-ROM discs are available now in most libraries. Sometimes they can be checked out for your use; other times they might be preinstalled in a library computer. If you check one out, you can slip the disc into a microcomputer in the same way that you would place a CD into your player at home. The on-screen directions include a list of references or pages of a text that will appear on the screen. You can print the material or download it onto your own floppy disk. You enter terms to find your material in the same way that you did for your bibliographic computer search. Obviously the more terms you plug in, the narrower the search will be. For example, the term "mythology" will yield much more material than "Mesoamerican mythology," and if you specify a particular kind of myth, such as "Mesoamerican creation myths," there will be even less material.

An online search is an exciting research experience and will help to immerse you in your subject. Even the titles that appear will, in themselves, be valuable in giving you ideas for your paper and suggest ways to develop and qualify your own thesis, and you will be confident to know that others before you have successfully explored the same area that you have chosen to investigate.

If you prefer to do a traditional search or supplement your online search because you enjoy browsing in your search for ideas, the following sources are particularly useful.

2. The Card Catalog

Most libraries now have a computer "card catalog," which is sometimes much more current than the material in the regular card catalog. It is important for you to speak to a librarian to find out the advantages of using the online computer catalog in your particular library before you proceed, since the computer may still not have all of the entries that have been stored in the traditional catalog.

Check to see how the materials in your library are cataloged. Some libraries have a single catalog in which you can look up author, title, or subject, all arranged in alphabetical order. Other libraries have a separate author catalog in which you can locate the card for a book if you know the author's name; a second catalog then contains alphabetized titles and subjects. Depending on your subject and your knowledge of it, you will look for books under a particular subject, a particular author, or a particular title. The author card for any book is considered the basic entry card. It is therefore important for you to know the significance of each entry on it:

EXAMPLE OF AN AUTHOR CARD IN THE CARD CATALOG

```
BL
311      Campbell, Joseph, 1904-1987
C263       The inner reaches of outer space:
1986     metaphor as myth and as religion.
         Joseph Campbell. New York: A. van
         der Marck Editions, c1986.
            155 p.: ill. (some col.); 25 cm.
            Includes bibliographical references
         and index.
            ISBN 0-912383-09-7


            1. Mythology.    2.  Religion.
         3. Metaphor—Religious aspects.
         I. Title
CLoBS    13 JUL 87    13008516    CLOSs1    8440776
```

NOTES: This card, like all author cards, identifies the book by the call number* in the upper left-hand corner.

The author's name is given in inverted order; the dates of birth and death are often included.

The first letter of the first word in each title is capitalized; but often, the entire title of the book is neither capitalized nor italicized on the catalog card. You must remember to capitalize the first and last words and then all other words of the title except for CAPs (conjunctions, articles, and prepositions); also remember to underline each word of the title separately to indicate italics.

If a bibliography is included in the book, the card will indicate it as this card does.

This book is cataloged also under its titles (after Roman numerals), its subjects (after the Arabic numbers), and if there were an editor and a translator they would be also listed after Roman numerals.

---

*See Library Classification Systems, pp. 136–138.

The way in which any book is cataloged or cross-filed will suggest other possible subjects for you to investigate.

3. Periodical Indexes

These will list magazine articles published on your subject; some of the most important indexes are listed below.

a. *The Reader's Guide to Periodical Literature* will list articles published in American magazines since 1900. It is a subject and author index with cross references; however, the subject index is the more complete.

NOTE: You will have to look in the volume for each year in which articles on your subject could have been written; for example, you would not look up *atomic energy* in the 1930 volume, but you would look up *mythology* in every volume.

Do not put information on your bibliography card the way it appears in *The Reader's Guide*. The abbreviations are explained at the front of each volume. The entry in the 1988 volume, which appears thus:

Triumph of Daedalus. J. Langford. Nat Geog 174:191–199 Aug '88

will be translated to a bibliography card thus:

```
Langford, John S.
"Triumph of Daedalus."
National Geographic August 1988:
191-199.
```

b. (1) *Social Science Index* (1907 to date) and

(2) *Humanities Index* (1907 to date) cover many learned and professional journals not included in *The Reader's Guide* and list foreign as well as American periodicals. They are extremely valuable for articles published since 1907. It is important to note that until 1974 these two indexes were combined into one index. That single index was titled *The International Index to Periodical Literature* from 1907 to 1966. In 1966 its name changed to

Social Science and Humanities Index. This lasted until 1974, when it was separated into the two indexes that now exist.

c. *Magazine Index* (1976 to date) is a microfilm index to a large number of general magazines and business periodicals.

d. *Poole's Index to Periodical Literature* is a subject index to British and American magazine articles published from 1802 to 1906.

e. *Nineteenth Century Reader's Guide to Periodical Literature* (1890–1899) is an index to fifty-one periodicals from 1890 to 1899. It gives the subject, author, and illustrator; some works of literature are listed under title entries. A special feature is the identification (wherever possible) of articles published anonymously.

f. *Book Review Digest* (1905 to date) gives reports on contemporary reviews and brief but useful information about the worth of books. There are excerpts from many of the reviews cited.

g. *MLA Bibliographies* (1921 to present) are yearly volumes listing essays in various periodicals devoted to language and literature (English, American, French, Spanish, Italian, German).

NOTE: Most libraries have a separate catalog index for periodicals, called a cardex, to help you find the periodicals in the library. You use the cardex to look up the title of the periodical and to ascertain that the library has it. If you have to find it elsewhere, look in *The Union List of Serials in Libraries of the U.S. and Canada, 1965*, which lists over 150,000 periodicals and where they can be found, so that your library can arrange to order a photocopy of the article you need.

There are more indexes listed on pp. 138–143.

4. Special Indexes

These include listings of books and magazines and newspaper articles on a variety of special subjects (such as education, religion, art, book reviews, medicine, engineering, biographies) and are usually found on open reference-room shelves. For example,

a. *The New York Times Index* (1913 to date) classifies all of the *Times* articles. It gives the date on which an event occurred, making it easier for you to look up information in other newspapers; its obituaries contain valuable biographical material about prominent people.

b. *Newspaper Index* (1972 to date) indexes four more major American newspapers: *The Washington Post*, *The Chicago Tribune*, *The Los Angeles Times*, and the *New Orleans Times-Picayune*. In 1976, indexes to the *Detroit News*, the *Houston Post*, the *San Francisco Chronicle*, and the *Milwaukee Journal* were added. The other major U.S. newspapers have their own indexes.

c. *Essay and General Literature Index* (1900–1933; supplements 1933 to date) lists essays and articles on given subjects found within collections of essays and miscellaneous books.

There are more indexes listed on pp. 138–143.

5. Bibliographies

There are many publications that are themselves merely bibliographies. Some are compiled on particular subjects; others, on individuals and their work. For example,

Sheehy, Eugene Paul, comp. *Guide to Reference Books*, 10th ed. (1986), divides his bibliography by subject (General Reference Works, The Humanities, Social Sciences, History and Area Studies, Pure and Applied Sciences); under each subject are numerous subcategories, each containing still more categories. Such an arrangement makes it possible to locate reference material on any subject easily and accurately.

Mark, Linda, ed. *Reference Sources* (1977 to date), divides her bibliography alphabetically according to the last name of the author and "provides indexing to all reference books which have been reviewed in over 140 journals." She lists "dictionaries, bibliographies, atlases, gazetteers, biographical dictionaries, chronologies, thesauri, indexes, statistical tables, directories" as well as "art catalogs (especially the catalog raisonné) and annual 'state of the art' reviews."

There are more bibliographies listed on pp. 138–143.

6. Encyclopedias

Many of these include excellent bibliographies in addition to the articles on particular subjects. For example, you will find bibliographies at the end of most articles in the *Encyclopaedia Britannica*. Check the card catalog for encyclopedias on special subjects, such as art, American history, American government, religion, physics, music, and so forth.

7. Sources That You Use

In most of your sources you will find clues to other relevant material by looking either in a bibliography at the back, in the footnotes, or in the material itself.

HOW TO WRITE YOUR BIBLIOGRAPHY CARDS

Record each entry or source on a separate 3 × 5 inch index card. Index cards enable you to organize and reorganize your sources in different ways, such as separating those you have already read from those you have not, arranging them alphabetically, topically, and chronologically, whereas a list on a sheet of paper does not.

Record the name of the author, the title, and the facts of publication accurately. The card, not the book, will be the source of information for the data you will use later in writing the footnotes and the final bibliography.

In order to save time and effort, you should make up your cards with whatever information you have, leaving lines and spaces to be completed when you have the actual book or other source in your hands.

On the back of the bibliography card put the call number and/or the place where you found out about this source. Also put any other information to which you might want to refer later. You will also use the back of the card to annotate your bibliography when you have seen the book. See pp. 52 and 127.

There are only two basic bibliographical forms:

1. There is a basic form for a source that is not part of a larger work.

2. There is a basic form for a source contained within a larger work.

FORM FOR A SOURCE THAT IS NOT PART OF A LARGER WORK

(Note: You need not have used or read the entire work.)

Campbell, Joseph.
The Inner Reaches of Outer Space: Metaphor
 as Myth and as Religion.
New York: Alfred van der Marck Editions,
1986.

1st line: author's name in inverted order
(If there are two or more authors, use the following form in example 3, 4, or 5).

end punctuation: period

2nd line: title of book
(Capitalize the first and last word and all other words except CAPs—short conjunctions, articles, and short prepositions; underline each word separately to indicate title as it appears on outside of book; underlining is a substitute for italics.)

end punctuation: period

3rd line: facts of publication
(Place of publication followed by colon and name of publisher.)

end punctuation: comma

NOTES: You must write the name of the publisher exactly as it appears on the title page, abbreviating and capitalizing only those words that are abbreviated and/or capitalized.

If more than one place of publication is given, use the first one listed unless it is in a foreign country; if only a foreign country is given, use it.

If the publisher is not given, write the abbreviation in brackets thus: [n.p.]

4th line: date of publication
(Whenever more than one date of publication or copyright is given, use the most recent one. If no date is given, write the abbreviation in brackets thus: [n.d.])

end punctuation: period

MODELS FOR A SOURCE THAT IS NOT PART OF A LARGER WORK

1. the basic form

```
Campbell, Joseph.
The Inner Reaches of Outer Space: Metaphor
    as Myth and as Religion.
New York: Alfred van der Marck Editions,
1986.
```

2. no author

```
Máscaras Mexicanas: de la Colección
    del Ing. Victor José Moya.
México: Dirección de Museos del
    Instituto Nacional de Antropología
    e Historia,
1974.
```

3. two authors

```
Markman, Roberta H., and Peter T. Markman.
The Flayed God: The Mesoamerican Mythological
    Tradition.
San Francisco: Harper San Francisco,
1992.
```

4. three authors

```
Broda, Johanna, Davíd Carrasco, and Eduardo
    Matos Moctezuma.
The Great Temple of Tenochtitlan: Center and
    Periphery in the Aztec World.
Berkeley: University of California Press,
1987.
```

5. more than three authors

Lothrop, Samuel K., and others.
Essays in Pre-Columbian Art and Archaeology.
Cambridge, Massachusetts: Harvard University
  Press,
1961.

NOTE: The author line may be thus:
         Lothrop, Samuel K., et al.

6. corporate authorship

Instituto Guerrerense de la Cultura.
Calendario de Fiestas del Estado de Guerrero.
Chilpancingo, Guerrero, México: Instituto
  Guerrerense de la Cultura,
1987.

7. an author and an editor

Campbell, Joseph.
The Power of Myth with Bill Moyers.
Ed. Betty Sue Flowers.
New York: Doubleday,
1988.

8. an author and a translator

Eliade, Mircea.
Images and Symbols.
Trans. Philip Mairet.
Kansas City, Missouri: Sheed Andrews
  and McMeel,
1961.

9. an author, an editor, and a translator

```
Neruda, Pablo.
A New Decade (Poems: 1958-1967).
Ed. Ben Belitt.
Trans. Ben Belitt and Alastair Reid.
New York: Grove Press,
1969.
```

10. an editor but no author

```
Apostolos-Cappadona, Diane, ed.
Symbolism, the Sacred, and the Arts.
New York: Crossroad,
1988.
```

NOTE: This form would be used when referring to an anthology as a whole rather than one of the works included in the anthology as well as for any other book with an editor but no author.

11. a translator and an editor but no author

```
Sullivan, Thelma D., trans.
A Scattering of Jades: Stories, Poems, and Prayers
  of the Aztecs.
Ed. T. J. Knab.
New York: Simon and Schuster,
1994.
```

NOTE: The translator precedes the editor on the title page of this book, and the bibliography card follows that order.

12. a compiler

```
Muser, Curt, comp.
Facts and Artifacts of Ancient
  Middle America.
New York: E. P. Dutton,
1978.
```

13. one volume is a multivolume set when all volumes have the same title

```
Budge, E. A. Wallis.
The Gods of the Egyptians or Studies
  in Egyptian Mythology, 2 vols.
1904;
rpt. New York: Dover Publications,
1969, Vol. 2.
```

NOTE: This is a modern reprint of a book originally published in 1904.
See example 18.

14. one volume in a multivolume set when each volume has a separate title

```
Coe, Michael D., and Richard A. Diehl.
The People of the River.
Vol. 2 of In the Land of the Olmec. 2 vols.
Austin: University of Texas Press,
1980.
```

15. a book in a series edited by one other than the author

```
Maclagen, David.
Creation Myths: Man's Introduction to
  the World.
In the Art and Imagination series.
Ed. Jill Purce.
London: Thames and Hudson,
1977.
```

NOTE: If the volumes were numbered, the third line would be thus:
Vol. 2 of Art and Imagination, as in example 14.

16. a book with a subtitle or secondary title

```
Hopper, Vincent F., ed. and trans.
Chaucer's Canterbury Tales: An Interlinear
   Translation.
Woodbury, New York: Barron's,
1970.
```

NOTE: Obviously Chaucer did not write a book with this title; there-
        fore this entry is correct for this book. If you quoted the intro-
        duction by Dr. Hopper, you would use this card for
        bibliography and for footnote. If you quoted the lines from
        Chaucer with the older spelling, your card would be thus:

16a.

```
Chaucer, Geoffrey.
"The Pardoner's Tale."
Chaucer's Canterbury Tales: An Interlinear
   Translation.
Ed. and trans. Vincent F. Hopper.
Woodbury, New York: Barron's,
1970.
```

17. an edition subsequent to the first edition

```
Coe, Michael D.
The Maya, 5th ed.
New York: Thames and Hudson,
1993.
```

18. a modern reprint of an older edition

```
Toor, Frances.
Mexican Popular Arts.
1939;
rpt. Detroit: Blaine Ethridge Books,
1973.
```

19. a pamphlet, bulletin, manual, or monograph

```
Mulryan, Lenore H.
Mexican Figural Ceramists and Their
  Work (Monograph Series, no. 16).
Los Angeles: Museum of Cultural History,
  University of California, Los Angeles,
1982.
```

NOTE: Omit parenthetical entry if the work is not one of a series.

20. a catalog of an exhibition

```
Billeter, Erika, ed.
The Blue House: The World of Frida Kahlo (an exhibit
  at the Schirn Kunsthalle, Frankfurt, March 6-May 23,
  1993 and The Museum of Fine Arts, Houston, June 6-
  August 29, 1993).
Frankfurt: Schirn Kunsthalle and Houston: Museum of
  Fine Arts,
1993.
```

21. a government document

```
U. S., Congressional Record.
80th Cong., 2nd Sess., 1948.
XCII, Part 6, 5539.
```

22. a dictionary

```
Webster's New Collegiate Dictionary.
Springfield, Massachusetts: G. & C.
  Merriam Company,
1984.
```

23. a record, audiotape, or compact disc

```
Brahms, Johannes.
Violin Sonatas Nos. 1-3.
Itzhak Perlman, violin, and Vladimir Ashkenazy, piano.
EMI/Angel, CDC 7 47403 2
Compact disc.
```

24. a film or videotape

```
Wings of Desire.
Wim Wenders, Director.
Orion Pictures Corp.,
1988.
```

25. a radio program

```
Tribute: Ernest von Dohnanyi.
KFAC (1330 AM, 92.3 FM), Los Angeles.
7-8 pm., 26 July 1988.
```

26. a television program

```
Moyers: Joseph Campbell and the Power
  of Myth, pt. 1.
KCET (Channel 28), Los Angeles. PBS.
10-11 p.m., 23 May 1988.
```

FORM FOR A SOURCE CONTAINED WITHIN A LARGER WORK

Jay, Gregory S.
"Knowledge, Power, and the Struggle for Representation."
<u>College English</u> January 1994:
9-29.

1st line: author's name in reverse order
> (For two or more authors, see examples 3, 4, and 5 in the preceding section.)

> end punctuation: period

2nd line: title of the article, essay, story, or poem (the contained work) enclosed in quotation marks
> (The title is capitalized except for CAPs—short conjunctions, articles, and short prepositions.)

> end punctuation: period before the closing quotation marks unless there is punctuation at that point as part of the title, in which case that punctuation is retained inside the quotation mark, and your period is omitted

3rd line: title of the larger work in which the article appears followed by the date of publication with the date first, if one is given, followed by the month and then the year, thus: 7 January 1994.

> NOTE: Some authorities distinguish between popular periodicals appearing weekly, biweekly, monthly, or bimonthly and scholarly journals, which are generally quarterly publications. When such a distinction is made, popular periodicals are referred to using the form we have given previously while scholarly journals are referred to by substituting the volume number and the year of publication for the date in the 3rd line, thus: <u>College English</u> 56 (1994)

> end punctuation: colon

4th line: the pages on which the particular work can be found
> (The abbreviations p. or pp. are not used. To give the pages on which a work occurs, use, for example:
> 9 to indicate that the work is complete on page 9;
> 9–29 to indicate that the work covers those twenty-one pages;

9–29, 84 to indicate that after the first twenty-one pages, the work concludes on page 84.

9–29, 84–86 to indicate that after the first twenty-one pages, the work continues from pages 84 to 86.)

end punctuation: period

MODELS FOR A SOURCE CONTAINED WITHIN A LARGER WORK

1. the basic form

```
Jay, Gregory S.
"Knowledge, Power, and the Struggle for Representa-
    tion."
College English January 1994:
9-29.
```

2. a periodical article with no author

```
"The Presidential Policy Scoreboard."
The World and I June 1988:
52-55.
```

3. a titled book review

```
Paz, Octavio.
"Food of the Gods."
Trans. Eliot Weinberger.
Review of The Blood of Kings by Linda
    Schele and Mary Ellen Miller.
The New York Review of Books 26 February 1987:
3-7.
```

4. an untitled book review

```
Neumann, Franke J.
Review of Masks of the Spirit: Image and Metaphor in
    Mesoamerica by Peter T. Markman and Roberta H.
    Markman.
Religious Studies Review April 1993:
179.
```

5. a newspaper article or editorial

```
Williams, Dan.
"400-Year Church Ties Cut by Ancient Mexican
   Tribe."
Los Angeles Times 5 July 1987:
I:1, 12-13.
```

NOTE: On the last line you must indicate the section (I in this case) in which the article appears as well as the page numbers. If there are various editions of the newspaper (Eastern Edition, Late Edition, and National Edition), you should specify the particular edition you are using after the date on line 3.

6. an essay (or other work) written by one person in an anthology edited by another

```
Eliade, Mircea.
"The Symbolism of Shadows in Archaic Religions."
Symbolism, the Sacred, and the Arts.
Ed. Diane Apostolos-Cappadona.
New York: Crossroad,
1988.
3-16.
```

7. an encyclopedia article

```
Bolle, Kees W.
"Myth and Mythology: The Nature, Functions, and
   Types of Myth."
The New Encyclopaedia Britannica: Macropaedia.
15th ed. 1986.
24: 710-720.
```

NOTE: Most articles are signed with only the initials of the author; at the front of the first volume is a list of the initials and full names of the contributors.

For an unsigned article, you would write nothing on the first line above the title of the article; leave the line blank because you may find the name of the author later.

Encyclopedias reverse titles and names in order to list articles alphabetically; you may or may not, but be consistent.

8. an introduction or limited part of a book by one other than the author

```
Campbell, Joseph.
"Introduction."
Masks of the Spirit: Image and Metaphor
  in Mesoamerica.
Peter T. Markman and Roberta H. Markman.
Berkeley: University of California Press,
1989.
ix-xix.
```

9. author of a work in a book in a series edited by others

```
Waardenburg, Jacques.
"Symbolic Aspects of Myth."
Myth, Symbol, and Reality.
Ed. Alan M. Olson.
Vol. 1 of The Boston University Studies in
  Philosophy and Religion.
Ed. Leroy S. Rouner.
Notre Dame, Indiana: University of Notre
  Dame Press,
1980.
41-68.
```

10. a reprint with critical comment by the editor

```
Wright, Andrew.
"Afterword."
Joyce Cary. The Horse's Mouth.
1944;
rpt. New York: Harper & Row Perennial Library,
1965.
347-353.
```

11. a casebook (a text for controlled research)

```
Stevenson, David.
"J. D. Salinger: The Mirror of Crisis."
The Nation 9 March 1957:
215-217;
rpt. If You Really Want to Know: A Catcher
  Casebook.
Ed. Malcolm M. Marsden.
Chicago: Scott, Foresman,
1963.
22-25.
```

NOTE: There are two ways to use a casebook: as an anthology of essays about a particular subject or as a library containing essays, which you will read and document as if you were reading the original. For the latter use, the original pagination appears in the casebook with slash marks wherever a page change occurred in the original. Check with your instructor about how to use the casebook; but it would never be wrong to use this model form.

FORMS FOR SPECIAL PROBLEMS

1. an interview

```
Markman, Roberta H.
Professor of Comparative Literature,
  California State University.
Personal interview on Mexican masks.
Long Beach, California,
April 16, 1994.
```

NOTE: Unless the person interviewed is well known, you should indicate through the use of the person's title why he or she is an authority on the subject of the interview.

2. an unpublished lecture

```
Markman, Peter T.
Professor of English, Fullerton College.
Class Lecture on Carlos Fuentes, The
   Death of Artemio Cruz.
Fullerton, California,
May 3, 1992.
```

3. a published lecture

```
Vonnegut, Kurt, Jr.
"Address to Graduating Class at Bennington
   College, 1970."
Wampeters, Foma and Granfalloons (Opinions).
New York: Dell,
1976.
159-168.
```

4. mimeographed or photocopied material

```
Brown, Betty Ann.
"Fiestas de Oaxaca."
1977.                        (mimeographed)
```

NOTE: Try to give as much identifying information as you can for
       material of this nature.

5. an unpublished thesis or dissertation

```
Markman, Roberta H.
"Mann's Joseph: From Dreamer to Artist."
Diss. Occidental College, Los Angeles,
1969.
```

6. a letter

```
Hemingway, Ernest.
A letter to Roberta Hoffman, dated August 12,
   1957, New York, and now in the archives of
   The University of Texas at El Paso Library,
   El Paso, Texas.
```

NOTE: In a footnote, simply: Unpublished letter from Ernest Hemingway to Roberta Hoffman, August 12, 1957.

7. the Bible or any well-known literary work that can be identified by book or scene plus lines or by chapter and verse

```
I Corinthians.
The Bible.
Revised Standard Version.
```

NOTE: The names of sacred scripture are neither underlined nor put in quotation marks. The translation of the Bible is assumed to be the King James Version unless another is named, as in the preceding example.

```
Milton, John.
Paradise Lost.
Book 1.
```

NOTE: The particular edition you used is not needed unless the work is a translation.

The name of a novel, a play, or a long poem would be underlined even if it is part of an anthology.

8. an abridgment

```
Style Manual (abridged), rev. ed.
Washington, D.C.: Government Printing Office,
1984.
```

9. record jacket notes

```
Mahler, Gustav.
Symphony No. 4.
Concertgebouw Orchestra, Amsterdam.
Cond. Bernard Haitink.
Philips, SAL 3729 802 888 LY.
Jacket notes.
```

10. a pamphlet included with a record or compact disc

```
Kostelanetz, Richard, and Editors of
  Time-Life Records.
"A Listener's Guide to the Recordings."
The Music of Today.
In The Story of Great Music series.
Time-Life Records, STL 145.
```

11. a lecture on a record or tape

```
Scherman, Thomas, narrator and cond.
"Musical Program Notes."
Beethoven's Symphony No. 5 in C Minor,
  Op. 67.
  The Philharmonic Promenade Orchestra of
  London. Cond. Sir Adrian Boult.
Vanguard, MARS 3005.
```

12. computer software

```
Weyh, John A., Joseph R. Crook, and Les N. Hauge.
The Mole Concept.
Pt. 2 of Concepts in General Chemistry.
Computer software.
COMPress. IBM PC.
```

13. a computer database

```
Sanchez, Thomas.
"The Rituals of the Maya."
American Journal of Anthropology 1993.
Dialog file 10, item 976-977.
```

HOW TO PREPARE
THE FINAL BIBLIOGRAPHY
(TO BE DONE AS PART OF STEP 10)

1. Take out all the bibliography cards to which you have referred in your footnotes. These cards constitute your working bibliography and are the only ones that will be used in making your final bibliography.

2. The number of sources you will list on the final bibliography should equal the number of first-entry footnotes in your paper. (These are the footnotes that give full bibliographical information the first time you document material from a source.)

3. Alphabetize your working bibliography cards according to the first letter that appears on the card, excepting *a*, *an*, and *the*. (The first letter may be in the author's name, the title of a magazine article, and so forth.) If the title begins with a Roman numeral, alphabetize according to the word that follows the Roman numeral; if the first word in the title is an Arabic number, alphabetize according to the way that number would be spelled. For example, "X Steps" would be alphabetized under S, but "10 Steps" would be alphabetized under *T*.

4. Since the bibliography page is a title page, the title, BIBLIOG-RAPHY, is centered and typed in capitals without underlining, and the page number is centered at the bottom of the page; it may be enclosed by parentheses or dashes.

5. The bibliography entries are single-spaced within each entry and double-spaced between entries. Write as a continuous sentence; do not divide into lines as on the cards. The second and subsequent lines of each entry are indented as for a paragraph (five

spaces); the punctuation on the bibliography card is copied exactly.

6. Bibliography entries are never numbered. Ordinarily, the bibliography is not divided into types of sources.

NOTE: There are many accepted styles for bibliographical citations, the two most popularly accepted ones being MLA (The Modern Language Association, 1988) and the author-date system used in the social and natural sciences such as anthropology, sociology, archaeology, chemistry, and physics. Rather than a bibliography, this format requires the preparation of a reference list using the author-date style, which differs from the MLA style bibliography in several important ways as illustrated on pp. 48–50.

There are also other formats that are acceptable in particular disciplines. Manuals of style published for many of the disciplines explain and illustrate the different formats preferred by scholars in the various areas. A list of some of the most widely used can be found on pp. 143–146. It might be wise to check with your instructor regarding the preferred form for your paper if there is a specialized form preferred. However, the most important point to remember is that it is essential to be consistent; use one or the other style throughout a single piece of work. (Note: it is essential for you to see also the author-date style footnoting changes if you are using that format for your reference list citations. See pp. 48–50 for a discussion of that format and comparisons with MLA.) The following section is based on the MLA style format.

BIBLIOGRAPHY*

Apostolos-Cappadona, Diane, ed. <u>Symbolism, the Sacred, and the Arts</u>. New York: Crossroad, 1988.

Billeter, Erika, ed. <u>The Blue House: The World of Frida Kahlo</u> (an exhibit at the Schirn Kunsthalle, Frankfurt, March 6-May 23, 1993 and The Museum of Fine Arts, Houston, June 6-August 29, 1993). Frankfurt: Schirn Kunsthalle and Houston: Museum of Fine Arts, 1993.

Bolle, Kees W. "Myth and Mythology: The Nature, Functions, and Types of Myth." <u>The New Encyclopaedia Britannica</u>: <u>Macropaedia</u>. 15th ed. 1986. 24: 710-720.

Brahms, Johannes. <u>Violin Sonatas Nos. 1-3</u>. Itzhak Perlman, violin, and Vladimir Ashkenazy, piano. EMI/Angel, CDC 7 47403 2. Compact disc.

Broda, Johanna, Davíd Carrasco, and Eduardo Matos Moctezuma. <u>The Great Temple of Tenochtitlan</u>: <u>Center and Periphery in the Aztec World</u>. Berkeley: University of California Press, 1987.

Brown, Betty Ann. "Fiestas de Oaxaca." 1977 (Mimeographed).

Budge, E. A. Wallis. <u>The Gods of the Egyptians or Studies in Egyptian Mythology</u>. 2 vols. 1904; rpt. New York: Dover Publications, 1969. Vol. 2.

Campbell, Joseph. <u>The Inner Reaches of Outer Space</u>: <u>Metaphor as Myth and as Religion</u>. New York: Alfred van der Marck Editions, 1986.

†---. "Introduction." <u>Masks of the Spirit</u>: <u>Image and Metaphor in Mesoamerica</u>. Peter T. Markman and Roberta H. Markman. Berkeley: University of California Press, 1989. ix-xix.

NOTE: All of these sources are reproduced as footnotes beginning on p. 85.

---

*This is a sample bibliography compiled from the sample bibliography cards shown on the preceding pages.

†These three hyphens followed by a period indicate that the author for this entry is the same as the author for the entry immediately above. Note, however, that hyphens are not used when the author is joined by another as in the following Coe entries.

---. The Power of Myth with Bill Moyers. Ed. Betty Sue Flowers. New York: Doubleday, 1988.

Chaucer, Geoffrey. "The Pardoner's Tale." Chaucer's Canterbury Tales: An Interlinear Translation. Ed. and trans. Vincent F. Hopper. Woodbury, New York: Barron's, 1970.

Coe, Michael D. The Maya. 5th ed. New York: Thames and Hudson, 1993.

Coe, Michael D., and Richard A. Diehl. The People of the River. Vol. 2 of In the Land of the Olmec. 2 vols. Austin: University of Texas Press, 1980.

I Corinthians. The Bible. Revised Standard Version.

Eliade, Mircea. Images and Symbols. Trans. Philip Mairet. Kansas City, Missouri: Sheed Andrews and McMeel, 1961.

---. "The Symbolism of Shadows in Archaic Religions." Symbolism, the Sacred, and the Arts. Ed. Diane Apostolos-Cappadona. New York: Crossroad, 1988. 3-16.

Hemingway, Ernest. A letter to Roberta Hoffman, dated August 12, 1957, New York, and now in the archives of The University of Texas at El Paso Library, El Paso, Texas.

Hopper, Vincent F., ed. and trans. Chaucer's Canterbury Tales: An Interlinear Translation. Woodbury, New York: Barron's, 1970.

Instituto Guerrerense de la Cultura. Calendario Fiestas del Estado de Guerrero. Chilpancingo, Guerrero, México: Instituto Guerrerense de la Cultura, 1987.

Jay, Gregory S. "Knowledge, Power, and the Struggle for Representation." College English January 1994: 9-29.

Kostelanetz, Richard, and Editors of Time-Life Records. "A Listener's Guide to the Recordings." The Music of Today. In The Story of Great Music series. Time-Life Records, STL 145.

Lothrop, Samuel K., and others. Essays in Pre-Columbian Art and Archaeology. Cambridge, Massachusetts: Harvard University Press, 1961.

Maclagen, David. <u>Creation</u> <u>Myths</u>: <u>Man's</u> <u>Introduction</u>
<u>to</u> <u>the</u> <u>World</u>. In the <u>Art</u> <u>and</u> <u>Imagination</u> series.
Ed. Jill Purce. London: Thames and Hudson, 1977.

Mahler, Gustav. <u>Symphony</u> <u>No</u>. <u>4</u>. Concertgebouw Orchestra, Amsterdam. Cond. Bernard Haitink. Philips, SAL
3729 802 888 LY. Jacket notes.

Markman, Peter T. Professor of English, Fullerton Col-
lege. Class Lecture on Carlos Fuentes, <u>The</u> <u>Death</u> <u>of</u>
<u>Artemio</u> <u>Cruz</u>. Fullerton College, Fullerton, Cali-
fornia. 3 May 1988.

Markman, Roberta H., and Peter T. Markman. <u>The</u> <u>Flayed</u>
<u>God</u>: <u>The</u> <u>Mesoamerican</u> <u>Mythological</u> <u>Tradition</u>. San
Francisco: Harper San Francisco, 1992.

Markman, Roberta H. "Mann's Joseph: From Dreamer to
Artist." Diss. Occidental College, Los Angeles. 1969.

---. Professor of Comparative Literature, California
State University, Long Beach. Personal interview on
Mexican masks. Long Beach, California. 16 April 1988.

<u>Máscaras</u> <u>Mexicanas</u>: <u>de</u> <u>la</u> <u>Colección</u> <u>del</u> <u>Ing</u>. <u>Victor</u>
<u>José</u> <u>Moya</u>. México: Dirección de Museos del Insti-
tuto Nacional de Antropología e Historia. 1974.

Milton, John. <u>Paradise</u> <u>Lost</u>. Book 1.

<u>Moyers</u>: <u>Joseph</u> <u>Campbell</u> <u>and</u> <u>the</u> <u>Power</u> <u>of</u> <u>Myth</u>, pt. 1.
KCET (Channel 28), Los Angeles. PBS. 10-11 p.m., 23
May 1988.

Mulryan, Lenore H. <u>Mexican</u> <u>Figural</u> <u>Ceramists</u> <u>and</u> <u>Their</u>
<u>Work</u> (Monograph Series, no. 16). Los Angeles:
Museum of Cultural History, University of California, Los Angeles, 1982.

Muser, Curt. comp. <u>Facts</u> <u>and</u> <u>Artifacts</u> <u>of</u> <u>Ancient</u> <u>Mid-</u>
<u>dle</u> <u>America</u>. New York: E. P. Dutton, 1978.

Neruda, Pablo. <u>A</u> <u>New</u> <u>Decade</u> <u>(Poems</u>: <u>1958-1967</u>). Ed.
Ben Belitt. Trans. Ben Belitt and Alastair Reid.
New York: Grove Press, 1969.

Neumann, Franke J. Review of <u>Masks</u> <u>of</u> <u>the</u> <u>Spirit</u>:
<u>Image</u> <u>and</u> <u>Metaphor</u> <u>in</u> <u>Mesoamerica</u> by Peter T. Mark-
man and Roberta H. Markman. <u>Religious</u> <u>Studies</u>
<u>Review</u> April 1993: 179.

Paz, Octavio. "Food of the Gods." Trans. Eliot Weinberger. Review of The Blood of Kings by Linda Schele and Mary Ellen Miller. The New York Review of Books 26 February 1987: 3-7.

"The Presidental Policy Scoreboard." The World and I June 1988: 52-55.

Sanchez, Thomas. "The Rituals of the Maya." American Journal of Anthropology. 1993. Dialog file 10, item 976-977.

Scherman, Thomas, narrator and cond. "Musical Program Notes." Beethoven's Symphony No. 5 in C Minor, Op. 67. The Philharmonic Promenade Orchestra of London. Cond. Sir Adrian Boult. Vanguard, MARS 3005.

Stevenson, David. "J. D. Salinger: The Mirror of Crisis." The Nation 9 March 1957: 215-217; rpt. If You Really Want to Know: A Catcher Casebook. Ed. Malcolm M. Marsden. Chicago: Scott, Foresman, 1963. 22-25.

Style Manual (abridged), rev. ed. Washington, D.C.: Government Printing Office, 1984.

Sullivan, Thelma D., trans. A Scattering of Jades: Stories, Poems, and Prayers of the Aztecs. Ed. T. J. Knab. New York: Simon and Schuster, 1994.

Toor, Francis. Mexican Popular Arts. 1939; rpt. Detroit: Blaine Ethridge Books, 1973.

Tribute: Ernest von Dohnanyi. KFAC (1330 AM, 92.3 FM), Los Angeles. 7-8 p.m., 26 July 1988.

U.S. Congressional Record. 80th Cong., 2nd Sess. 1948. XCII, Pt. 6, 5539.

Vonnegut, Kurt, Jr. "Address to Graduating Class at Bennington College, 1970." Wampeters, Foma and Granfalloons (Opinions). New York: Dell, 1976. 159-168.

Waardenburg, Jacques. "Symbolic Aspects of Myth." Myth, Symbol, and Reality. Ed. Alan M. Olson. Vol. 1 of The Boston University Studies in Philosophy and Religion. Ed. Leroy S. Rouner. Notre Dame, Indiana: University of Notre Dame Press, 1980. 41-68.

Webster's New Collegiate Dictionary. Springfield, Massachusetts: G. & C. Merriam Company, 1984.

Weyh, John A., Joseph R. Crook, and Less N. Hauge. <u>The Mole</u> Concept. Pt. 2 of <u>Concepts</u> <u>in</u> <u>General</u> Chemistry. Computer software. COMPress. IBM PC.

Williams, Dan. "400-Year Church Ties Cut by Ancient Mexican Tribe." <u>Los</u> <u>Angeles</u> <u>Times</u> 5 July 1987: I:1, 12-13.

<u>Wings</u> <u>of</u> <u>Desire</u>. Wim Wenders, Director. Orion Pictures Corp., 1988.

Wright, Andrew. "Afterword." Joyce Cary. <u>The</u> <u>Horse's</u> <u>Mouth</u>. 1944; rpt. New York: Harper & Row/Perennial Library, 1965. 347-353.

AUTHOR–DATE SYSTEM (APA STYLE)
(USED PRIMARILY IN THE SOCIAL AND NATURAL SCIENCES)

In the author–date style both the bibliographical form and the form for citing the source in the text differ from the MLA style illustrated previously.

FORM FOR BIBLIOGRAPHY USING THE AUTHOR–DATE SYSTEM

The appropriate title for the page is REFERENCES, LIST OF REFERENCES, or WORKS CITED; it may also be BIBLIOGRAPHY. For a book or article with one author, this format requires that you cite only the initials of the author's first name and capitalize only the first word of the title and subtitle. The year of publication is placed immediately following the author's name:

Campbell, J. 1986. *The inner reaches of outer space: Metaphor as myth and as religion.* New York: Alfred van der Marck Editions.

Jay, G. 1994. "Knowledge, power, and the struggle for representation." *Coll. Eng* 56: 9–29.

For a second book by the same author, the author's name is replaced by seven spaces of the underline key instead of the three hyphens of the MLA form.

For a book with two authors, invert the surname of the first author and separate the names with a comma followed by *and*.

Markman, R., and P. Markman. 1992. *The flayed god: The Mesoamerican mythological tradition*. San Francisco: Harper San Francisco.

See the following item #4 for the form of reference lists in which there are many works by the same author(s).

The major differences between the author–date system and MLA styles can be summarized as follows:

1. Author–date entries substitute initials for the first names of authors or editors, whereas MLA style cites first names.

2. Author–date style capitalizes only the first word of a book or article title or subtitle and proper names and article titles are not placed in quotes, whereas in MLA style all major words in titles are capitalized and article titles are enclosed in quotation marks. Both capitalize journal titles.

3. In citing dates, author–date format places the date after the author's name whereas in MLA style, the dates are placed with information about publication.

4. In the author–date style, if the bibliography is long with many works by one author, the author's name is given on a separate line followed by the dates of publication in chronological order and the publication information. If two or more works by the same author were published in the same year, each is identified by a lowercase letter: 1987a and 1987b.

   Campbell, J.
   1969   *The flight of the wild gander*. New York: The Viking Press.
   1974   *The mythic image*. Princeton: Princeton University Press.
   1986   *The inner reaches of outer space: Metaphor as myth and as religion*. New York: Alfred van der Marck Editions.

(See pp. 43–48 for the MLA style format.)

FORM FOR PARENTHETICAL DOCUMENTATION USING THE AUTHOR–DATE SYSTEM

Parenthetical reference notes for the author–date style include the author's last name and the year of publication followed by a comma and a page reference: (Campbell 1987, 60). If any of this information is given in the text, it may be omitted from the parenthetical reference. If two or more works by the same author were published in the same year, each is identified by a lowercase letter: 1987a and 1987b; a short title to distinguish between the works is not used.

(See pp. 81–83 for a discussion of parenthetical references using the MLA style-format.)

STEP

TAKE NOTES FROM RELEVANT SOURCES

Good notecards are the key to a well-developed, easy-to-read paper and will facilitate the actual writing of your paper. In fact, to a great extent, the notecards actually determine the course of your research and the final paper you will write.

The order in which you take notes will not be the order in which you will use them in your paper; therefore, it is important to keep them independent of each other and clear in meaning to you. Each notecard must be precisely identified as to source and page so that you can document the information if you use it in your paper; or if you are working with sources that are not printed matter, be sure to indicate how and where you obtained your information.

There are times when you will need to use information from a periodical or a book that does not circulate and you may not have time to take all the notes that would be valuable to you. You might find it helpful to photocopy material to reread and work with at home. Be sure that you (1) make a copy of the title page and copyright page for a book and the publication-data page of a periodical and staple it to the material you copy and (2) that you do not cut off the page numbers as you copy them.

The amount and kind of information you write on each card will vary with the type of note you take, which will be guided not only by the information you record but also by the way you think it might be used in your paper. (The section marked "Kinds of Notecards," pp. 54

to 63, will indicate possible varieties.) Follow this outlined procedure and your notetaking will be orderly and rewarding.

HOW TO TAKE NOTES

1. Write your notes on 4 × 6-inch cards in pen if not typed because pencil smudges when cards rub against each other and becomes illegible. If you use a computer to take some of your notes, be sure they are printed on paper that is the same size as the cards.

2. Write on *one* side of the card only.

3. Before you take a single note from any source, take out the bibliography card that you have prepared for that source. Check each item of the bibliography card against the source in your hands to make sure that you have the complete and correct facts concerning that particular source. Fill in any information you did not already have on the card.

   Put a check mark on the bottom corner of the card to remind yourself that you have checked the accuracy of the bibliographical information directly from the book itself (and not from someone else's bibliography that may or may not be accurate).

   Annotate your bibliography by making brief remarks on the back of the card. Make notes about whether the book has a chapter or just a few pages that will be useful to you, such as "chapter 3 (pp. 24–41) has genealogy and complete list of Egyptian gods. A time chart could be useful. Rest deals with history and not useful for me." Note also if the information is well documented from reliable sources, if it is gathered from original research, and if it has an extensive bibliography. Brief notes such as these will remind you later of what kind of information each book or article contains. You may not realize in your early notetaking stages that certain information would be useful, but later you might find that it would fit right into your argument, and you will save a lot of time by referring to your annotated bibliography cards to remind you of where you saw what.

4. Before you begin to take any notes, write the author's last name on the left corner of the top line. Leave the right side of the top line blank for outline label or slug (*see* STEP 6). If you use other

books by the same author, you will need to differentiate among them by using the date of publication in parentheses after the author's name and by using an *a* or *b* after the date if there are two books published in the same year (i.e., Smith 1990a and Smith 1990b). If you are using books by authors with the same last name, put the first name after the last (i.e., Smith, Henry and Smith, George).

5. Write only one idea from one source on each card. Make it a habit not to continue to a second card. Break the material into separate ideas. Never use a single card for notes from two sources. Notecards should be able to be organized in any order. The order will be determined by your outline later.

6. Put the page number in a circle before the first word on the note-card. If one idea is discussed on several pages in the source, indicate each page change by encircling the new page number before writing down the first word taken from that page. For example: ⓺⓺ "There are several factors... ⓷⓻ The first factor...and ⓸⓪ the second factor are important."

7. Early in your reading you will discover the need to adjust your reading speed to fit the material; not all printed material will be of equal value to you. When Bacon wrote that "some books are to be tasted, others to be swallowed, and some few to be chewed and digested," he could have been writing instructions to the student engaged in research. You must determine the relevance of each new source to your thesis and then decide how you will read it and what notes or information you need to take from it.

8. When you find the information that you want to use, decide what kind of note will suit your needs. Although some experienced researchers, particularly when they do not know exactly how they will use the information, prefer to take almost all notecards as direct quotes with plans to convert the information later into a paraphrase, summary, or other type of note, we suggest that for a short paper you use either paraphrase or summary to avoid problems of plagiarism. If you do take notes that are directly quoted, it is crucial that you use quotation marks on your card so that you will remember—even in the case of quoting just a few words—that the words within the quotation marks are not your own. It is essential to be accurate and concise in taking your

notes in order to avoid the problem of plagiarism. (*See* "Plagiarism: A Step to Avoid" pp. 120–127.)

9. As you take your notes, you should enter the labels or slugs *in pencil* on the right-hand side of the top line of your notecard (*see* STEP 6 now). The label you enter will normally be one of the items (or a subpoint under it) from your preliminary outline.

10. Do not hesitate to take duplicating or contradictory notes; you may need them to defend your thesis later or to have a choice of sources to quote.

11. You do not need to document facts of common knowledge, such as "some people who have the AIDS virus are not aware that they have it." However, if you use a source that interprets or analyzes that fact, documentation is essential. Of course, your own analysis or interpretation or illustration of that fact need not be documented.

KINDS OF NOTECARDS

All notes for the following illustration are taken from the Preface that is reproduced following the sample notecards at the end of STEP 5. That Preface is part of the master's thesis that is identified on the bibliography card reproduced on page 65.

It is essential to be accurate and concise in taking notes in order to avoid the problem of plagiarism. (*See* "Plagiarism: A Step to Avoid," pp. 120–127.)

A. **Direct quotation (verbatim).** Be accurate; copy from the printed page exactly. Do not change the punctuation or the spelling; if there is an error, copy it and add sic in brackets to indicate that the error was found in the original. Enclose within double quotation marks all that you copy. (See card A.)

   Direct quotations are valuable especially if the impact of the material would be lost by summarizing or paraphrasing it or if the author has made his point in such a way that any other language would destroy its meaning.

A

```
Markman
```

 "Later I realized that these images are also found in primitive art. Mitchell explains that visual representation is 'not radically distinct from language,' and Elizabeth Abel contends that the underlying concepts of myth and art are similar in that both express a 'common inner source whose subject matter changes but whose nature is the same.'"

A

When there are double quotation marks within the passage, they will become single marks within your double ones. See card I if you think you might use the quotes from Mitchell and Abel in your final paper.

B. Direct quotation of all or part of a passage with allowable changes:

   1. Ellipsis (the omission of a word or passage indicated by three periods with a space before and after and between each period). See card B1.

B1

```
Markman
```

 "But gradually I realized that...those marvelous tales were metaphorical expressions of essential aspects of the human condition."

B1

When any part of the quoted material depends for its meaning on a word or passage that you have not included, either omit that item by using ellipsis marks or else add inside of brackets an explanation of the phrase, so that later you will know the reference and you will be aware that it is not part of the quoted section of the original text. See card B2.

2. Brackets (used to enclose material you add within the quotation or to indicate a change in the form of some word). See card B2.

B2

Markman

 "But gradually I realized that on another level [other than being fascinated by the narratives and sense of magic] those marvelous tales were metaphorical expressions of essential aspects of the human condition."

B2

The allusion to levels appeared in an earlier passage and needs to be inserted here if you are concerned with the various levels on which mythology is being considered.

3. Certain limited changes without brackets:

a. Capitals may be made lowercase (or vice versa) if such a change will enable you to use the quotation as part of your own sentence. Lowercase letters may be capitalized if you want to begin a sentence in the middle of a sentence from your source. See card B3.

B3

Markman

 "When man attempts to explain the unknown, he is likely to depend on imagery from what he does know or on archetypal images which come out of his own inner experiences."

B3

In the original, *when* was not capitalized. Remember, von Franz must be given credit in a footnote to indicate that Markman was quoting this passage from her.

b. A final (or internal) punctuation mark within a quoted passage may be altered or omitted for the same reason. Or you may add a period if you terminate a quotation before the end of the sentence. See card B4.

B4

Markman

  "Each social group had obviously developed a mythology by which it could understand the basic experiences of its existence."

B4

In the original there was a comma after *existence*. An ellipsis is not needed here to show that sentence continues. Nothing from the text is omitted here nor is there any change in the context of the quoted passage.

c. Tense may be altered to make the material fit the context of your own paper. See card B5.

B5

Markman

  Markman agreed with von Franz that "when man attempted to explain the unknown, he was likely to depend on imagery from what he knew or on archetypal images which came out of his own inner experiences."

B5

In the original *attempted* was present tense; *was* was present tense; *knew* was *does know* and *came* was present tense.

d. Italics in the original will be indicated by underlining. If, for emphasis, you want to italicize words not italicized in the original, so indicate after the quotation by parentheses in which you say (Italics mine). See card B6.

B6

Markman

 Markman identifies three stages of interest in mythology: she was fascinated at first by "the dramatic action of the narratives and the aura of magic," later by the "metaphorical expression," and finally by the function and methodology of mythology and art which have many "common denominators." The world they depict "may not be literally true," but both verbal and visual forms do capture the "essential truth" of the human condition. (Italics mine)

B6

In the original the five quoted phrases were in different sentences and not necessarily in that order.

NOTE: These five short quoted passages would be documented in a single footnote.

C. Précis. This is a careful rewrite in your own words, usually about one-third the length of the original. In writing a precis, you are actually composing part of your paper. It is important to maintain the style, the point of view, and the tone of the original without using exact words or phrases from your source. See card C.

C

Markman

 Markman was fascinated by the stories and magic of mythology. Later she realized they were metaphors by which life's mysteries were described and understood. Daily experiences and primordial images in man's psyche provided the sources of the imagery for these myths which, although not scientifically true, show valid insight into some basic areas of the human condition. Von Franz, Mitchell, and Abel are convinced that the visual arts share this function and manifest similar imagery. A comparative study of visual and verbal expression in primitive society would be instructive. (P)

C

A capital *P* in parentheses will remind you later that the words are your own; you would then footnote the idea but would not put quotation marks around it. Do the same for paraphrases.

D. Summary. This kind of note states in your own words and/or condenses the basic ideas of a long passage, chapter, or even whole book. See card D.

D

Markman

 Verbal and visual expression serve similar functions with comparable imagery by which primitive societies have conceptualized their basic life experiences.

E. Outline. This kind of note reduces to organized form the basic information in a paragraph, page, or chapter. See card E.

E

Markman

 Myth and art are the media by which societies express basic beliefs.
Through myth their beliefs are expressed in
verbal metaphor. Through art their beliefs
are expressed in visual metaphor.
Ultimately the medium and the imagery are
comparable.

F. **Paraphrase.** Use this with caution, for it is easy to be careless and end up being a plagiarist. You will avoid this danger if you read the passage well, close the book, and then write your paraphrase from memory. (*See* "Plagiarism: A Step to Avoid," pp. 120–127.) The paraphrase (see card F) is good to use

1. when you need to simplify some pedantic or esoteric passage;

2. when you rephrase or clarify another's definition or explanation;

3. when you put the lines of a poem into your own words.

F

Markman

 Markman states that the narratives and the
magical aura of mythology are fascinating.
In addition, one can read myths as a
metaphoric expression of some important
beliefs about life; they help a society to
understand the mysteries of birth, death,
and the relationship of man and nature.
Even though these stories are not scientifically true, they do tell some basic truths
about the human condition. Von Franz says
that the imagery comes from the experience
of everyday life or from the primordial

> images of man's psyche. Markman found that
> Mitchell and Abel documented her observa-
> tion that primitive art also serves this
> function and utilizes the same kinds of
> imagery. She thinks a comparable study of
> the verbal and visual arts of primitive
> societies would be valuable. (P)

NOTE: Indicate the beginning of any paraphrase by informally men-
tioning the author and/or title, and be sure to note when other
authors need to be given credit for an idea, as with von Franz,
Mitchell, and Abel. See card F.

G. Combination note. While you are making your notes, you will
occasionally find it advisable to weave a quotation into a sentence
of your own to remind you of how you intended to use the material or to enable you to use the card intact in your rough draft. The
only danger lies in possible carelessness: be sure to make clear
(even exaggerated) quotation marks around the quoted part of the
sentence to distinguish it from your own words. See card G.

G

> Markman
>
> Mythology provided a means by which "each
> social group...could understand the basic
> experiences of its existence, such as cre-
> ation, nature, and death." Markman wanted
> "to investigate the common denominators of
> the verbal and visual expressions" by com-
> paring primitive art with mythology.

H. Quotation taken from footnote. It is important to indicate
the source quoted in the footnote of the material you are reading; then any error in the quotation or publication data will be
that author's, not yours. His or her source will not be included in
your own bibliography unless you have also used it as one of your
own sources. See card H.

H

> Markman
>
> Markman states that Marie-Louise von Franz, *Patterns of Creativity Mirrored in Creation Myth* (Zürich: Spring Publications, 1978), p. 5, "based her conclusions [regarding the sources of imagery] on the images she has found on maps of antiquity."

I. Quotation of a quote. Use this rarely. If a quotation is valuable enough to quote, you should try to see the original from which the quote was taken. However, since some material used by other writers might be difficult for you to obtain, this kind of note might be necessary. The source quoted by the author you read will not be included in your bibliography unless you have actually used it as one of your own sources. See card I.

I

> Markman
>
> "The underlying concepts of myth and art are similar in that both express a 'common inner source whose subject matter changes but whose nature is the same.'"

NOTE: If you used this sentence in your paper, your footnote would cite Markman as your source, not Abel. The identification at the top of the card already indicates that Markman is your source, but you need to note that she was quoting Abel. Then add bibliographical information about Abel's article; you may be able to locate and use it yourself.

J. Critical. You may wish to make an evaluation of the material you are reading or to write down your own ideas about it. This kind of note will remind you of judgments made during your reading. See card J.

J

Markman
_____

 Markman does not indicate clearly what the focus of the comparative study will be.

    K. Synopsis or condensation. This is a summary of narrative material (i.e., a motion picture, a novel, a play, a narrative poem, etc.) No illustration card is given.

NOTE: Every completed notecard (*see* STEPS 6 and 7) should have five items on it:

    1. source identification

    2. page number in a circle

    3. the note itself

    4. quotation marks around verbatim quotes OR the letter *P* to indicate your personal wording or paraphrase

    5. the label (slug) or an outline symbol (*see* STEP 6.)

PUNCTUATION WITH QUOTATION MARKS—Remember these rules:

All commas and periods go *inside* the closing quotation marks.

All other punctuation goes inside *only* when it is a part of the quoted matter.

PREFACE FROM WHICH NOTECARDS WERE TAKEN

The following reproduced Preface is the source for the sample note-cards given in the previous section.

PREFACE

My earliest attraction to mythology was based on a
fascination with the dramatic action of the narratives and the aura of magic that pervades the world
in which that action takes place. But gradually I
realized that on another level those marvelous
tales were metaphorical expressions of essential
aspects of the human condition. Each social group
had obviously developed a mythology by which it
could understand the basic experiences of its existence, such as creation, nature, and death. Although
their mythological stories might not be literally
true, they do by analogy capture the essential truth
both of the society's world view and of the basic
nature of being. Von Franz says that when man
attempts to explain the unknown, he is likely to
depend on imagery from what he does know or on
archetypal images which come out of his own inner
experiences.[1] Later I realized that these images are
also found in primitive art. Mitchell explains that
visual representation is "not radically distinct
from language,"[2] and Elizabeth Abel contends that
the underlying concepts of myth and art are similar
in that both express a "common inner source whose
subject matter changes but whose nature is the
same."[3] I was challenged to investigate the common
denominators of the verbal and visual expressions
of these insights and to do a comparative study of
their metaphoric forms.

---

[1]Marie-Louise von Franz, Patterns of Creativity
Mirrored in Creation Myths (Zürich: Spring Publications, 1978), 5. Von Franz bases her conclusions on
the images she has found on maps of antiquity.

[2]W. J. T. Mitchell, "Spatial Form in Literature:
Toward a General Theory," The Language of Images,
ed. W. J. T. Mitchell (Chicago: University of
Chicago Press, 1980), 296. Mitchell reinforces his
point with a quote from Ludwig Wittgenstein's
Philosophical Investigations: "A picture held us

captive. And we could not get outside it, for it lay in our language and language seemed to repeat it to us inexorably." (271).

[3]Elizabeth Abel, "Redefining the Sister Arts: Beaudelaire's Response to the Art of Delacroix," The Language of Images, ed. W. J. T. Mitchell (Chicago: University of Chicago Press, 1980), 41.

BIBLIOGRAPHICAL CARD FOR PREFACE

Markman, Roberta H.
"The Metaphoric Vision in Mythology and Art."
Master's thesis,
California State University, Long Beach,
1994.

STEP

LABEL NOTECARDS
AND REVISE
WORKING OUTLINE

While you are taking your notes, you will observe that they can be categorized under several general headings. Often you will see that these headings coincide with the various units of your preliminary outline; on the other hand, they often suggest topics that need to be added to your outline. Remember, as you read, that you will not only be revising your preliminary outline but also reevaluating and reformulating your thesis statement in the light of your increased knowledge and accumulated information.

The items of your preliminary outline will provide the labels or slugs which you will write in pencil on the top lines of your notecards; pencil is better than ink here because you may want to change your label if you find later that a particular note could be used better under another heading. Some material cannot be categorized easily; leave these notecards to be labeled later. Some notes will be particularly good as part of an introduction or a conclusion; use "intro." or "concl." as the slugs for these. Some notes will obviously not belong at all; mark these with an X and put them aside for the time being.

As you come closer to finishing your research, you will find that your notecards fall into four or five general categories, and these might turn out to be quite different from your original points for a temporary outline. You should now study your notecards and group them under general categories. Simply separate your cards into stacks, according to the ideas on them. This may take considerable time, but it is time well spent for in this way you will determine the organization of your entire paper.

If, for example, you were writing a paper to compare the visual and verbal metaphors by which various cultures have attempted to understand the basic phenomena of life, you might see that your cards can easily be divided into the basic areas of life that are most frequently the concern of both mythology and art. These might include the expression of the process of creation, the relationship of the individual (microcosm) to the universal (macrocosm), the conception of death and an afterlife, and so forth. These classifications could then become the Roman numerals for your outline. Then you would further divide your cards into several subpoint labels, and one notecard might be labeled thus:

```
Markman              God related to life/death—also water
```

(27)   In many myths "Death is presented as a fig-
        ure opposite, but complementary to, the Cre-
        ator as source of life." Sometimes a twin
        who becomes God of the underworld.
(28)   Water is also important to creation and yet
        is often the means of destruction of the
        world.

NOTE: This card would go with III A 1 on the outline for the paper, page 101.

If, on the other hand, you were doing your research on the subject of smog control, you might find that your notecards would fall into such categories as causes of the smog problem, manifestations of the smog problem, effects of smog on various aspects of the environment, solutions to the problem of smog control. These general classifications would then supply the Roman numerals for your outline.

You may find other possibilities for different classifications by studying the following as they might relate to your subject. If you think you have sufficient information on only one aspect that is suggested, then select that narrower area for your paper and break that down further to create your outline.

problem—cause—effect—solution
social causes—political causes—economic causes—psychological
   causes

the various effects (or solutions or manifestations) of some problem
different kinds of irony or values or attitudes
different (or similar) characteristics of something or someone
different ways of evaluating your topic
different advantages (or disadvantages) of a particular method,
    machine, approach, or process

Comparing and contrasting is a particularly instructive and creative
way of organizing a documented paper. It enables the student to come
to valuable conclusions by "measuring" one idea or area in terms of
another. There are, however, three basic considerations to keep in mind:

1. Be sure before you begin that the two areas to be compared and
   contrasted have just enough in common to make them comparable without being ridiculously obvious or impossibly unrelated.

2. Be sure to qualify your points by telling to what extent and how
   one area is different from the other, thus avoiding the risk of
   overstating your case to the point of losing its credibility.

3. Be sure to compare and contrast the two areas *point by point*
   rather than discussing *all* of one area and then *all* of the other,
   thereby forcing your readers to determine the similarities and differences for themselves.

REVISING YOUR OUTLINE

(*See also* TEMPORARY OUTLINE, STEP 3, pp. 12–13 and STEP 7, #2
on pp. 70–71.)

After you have found a way to divide your notecards into separate
larger classifications, mark with a Roman numeral I all the cards in the
classification you think you will discuss first in your paper; use a II for
those you will discuss in the second part, and so on. Then take all the
ones you have marked with numeral I and, considering them as material for a separate essay, determine into what categories you can further divide those ideas. For example, you might find that the pile of
cards marked I, because they all deal with the causes of the smog problem (#2 in the preceding list), contain some that deal with problems
related to industry, others deal with problems related to transportation,
others with problems related to private homes. These would be divided
into IA, IB, and IC. Then you would consider each of these sections
separately. You might decide that those cards marked IA or IB do not
need further division, but that those marked IC need to be divided into

such categories as road transportation and air transportation, and you would mark the cards appropriately IC 1 and IC 2.

Remember in your outlining that you can never have a I without at least a II, nor an A without at least a B, nor a 1 without at least a 2, since logically nothing can be divided into fewer than two parts (not even apples.) And your outline actually represents a division of ideas for the purpose of analyzing a subject in an organized fashion. At first, then, your notecards might have a label or slug like the preceding example; but once your outline is really set, you can save time by simply using the outline number instead.

Now you are ready to write the outline in its final form, taking care to word the items so that all Roman numerals (subdivisions of your thesis) are worded to be parallel in logic and in grammar; all the letter entries (A, B, C) are stated as parallel subdivisions of the Roman numeral under which they appear; and all the numbered entries (1, 2, 3) are logically and grammatically parallel subdivisions of the statement made in the letter under which they appear.

Before you can decide that you have finished your note-taking, you should examine your notecards and your revised outline to determine if you have adequate material for all the areas that are important to your thesis or a particular part of its proof. This evaluation will direct any subsequent note-taking to those specific topics for which you need more information, and you will then take only those notes that you know you will use. If you do take more notes on some new material that necessitates the inclusion of a new point, be sure to change your outline to include it.

ERRORS FREQUENTLY FOUND IN STUDENT OUTLINES

There are two major problems often made in constructing the outline that will result in problems with the paper itself:

1. The thesis is too broad and cannot be adequately "proved" in the space limitation of the paper. *See* STEP 3.

2. The major points do not relate directly to the thesis, and the subpoints do not "break down" the major point above it. Consequently, there will be material in the final paper that does not relate to the thesis. Just because you have some information on a notecard does not mean it will be relevant to your point. *See* "Revising Your Outline," above.

STEP

WRITE THE FIRST
DRAFT

Although you will never have the feeling that you have finished your note-taking to your satisfaction and you will never lose the feeling that you could do a much better job if you could examine "just one more source," the time for writing the first draft inevitably comes.

1. Check your thesis; be sure that it states as specifically as possible in a simple declarative sentence exactly what the material you have gathered adds up to.

2. Check your outline; be sure that each subtopic is directly relevant to the more general topic above it and, finally, that each major topic is directly relevant to the thesis. Make each item parallel to every other item both logically and grammatically. (That is, in a sentence outline, which is definitely preferable to a topic outline, be sure that each item is stated in a full sentence; in a topic outline, be sure that all terms are stated in parallel parts of speech, which are also parallel logically.) Check to see that no item overlaps another. Remember that no item can be divided into just one part: every I must have a II, every A must have a B, every 1 must have a 2, and so forth. Check to see that you have arranged the items of your outline in logical order: order of space or time, order of importance, order of complexity, and so forth. REMEMBER: Just as it is better and more advantageous to detect the faults in a floor plan for a house on the blueprint

than it is to find them in the finished building, so it is easier and more advantageous to find the errors of your logic and organization in your outline than it is to find them in your finished paper.

3. Your outline should now be ready for you to write in its final form if you have followed the instructions in STEP 6. (*See* sample outline STEP 10 pp. 100–101.) If you have some notecards you cannot use (there are inevitably a few), do not destroy them; put them away, for you may be able to use them in writing some other paper in the future.

4. Do not begin by writing your introduction. Wait to write that when your paper is completed and you can see what you are introducing. Start now by putting on paper as quickly as possible the overall information you wish to convey about your major points and their subdivisions. Save the fun of polishing your style until later; first you must capture your ideas on paper so you can think about them.

Develop your first point first. Arrange the notecards for your first Roman numeral to correspond with the order in that part of your outline and plunge right in as if you were writing a short essay with Roman numeral I as your thesis.

5. The complete thesis should appear early in the paper so that your reader knows where you are going. Topic sentences (usually a point on your outline) generally come at the beginning of paragraphs and then they are developed by giving examples, descriptions, and facts and figures taken from your research. Be sure that all the quoted or paraphrased material is carefully analyzed so that the reader knows how and why you are using that particular material to make your point.

6. Write on one side of the paper only and skip a line between each line of your writing so that you can cross out poor or awkward phrases and add better wording without unnecessary recopying later when you revise. If you type your draft, triple space for the same reason. If you are using a computer, you can move the material around very easily, of course.

7. Try to use direct quotations very sparingly in your paper. Use them only when there is no other way the material can be stated and when the exact words of the author must be used to make your point. Copy the quotations very carefully, using identical punctuation and wording of the original if you are writing on a computer. However, if you are typing or writing out your first draft and you are using a direct quote, simply staple or clip the notecard on which it is written to the place where it belongs in your text. This will save time and avoid the possibility of inaccuracy as a result of recopying.

It is very important to learn how to "weave" quoted or paraphrased material so that it becomes a part of your own text. Try not to use the colon to introduce any quotation unless it is long enough to block (i.e., one over three lines in length); otherwise, weave quotations into your own sentences so that a person hearing the paper read aloud would be unable to tell where a quote actually begins or ends. Make all quoted material sound like an integral part of your whole work; this means you must pay attention to point of view and tense, and provide necessary lead-ins and transitions to the material. Not only does integrating the source material into your text add to the general unity and fluency of your writing, it also serves the even more important purpose of indicating the relevance of that source material to the content of your paper. In other words, before using a quoted or paraphrased passage, think of why you are using it or of what purpose it serves in your paragraph; then weave it into your text by indicating some relevance, which you clarify in your own wording. It will then be valuable to your proof of thesis, and its implications will be clear to your reader.

For example, in the following sentence from a discussion of Gerhart Hauptmann's play *The Weavers*, there is no doubt about the significance of the quotation used:

> The formula for success, which according to Master Wiegand is "cunning, quickness, and ruthless determination" (30), had to be exposed and challenged.

Poorly used, the quotation might be inserted without any indication of relevance to the purpose of the paper, which (as here) might be a study of the values questioned in the play. An example of the same quotation, ineptly used, might read thus:

> Master Wiegand said: "Cunning, quickness, and ruthless determination are necessary" (30).

Your reader would naturally wonder, "Necessary for what?" You might profit at this point by studying the sample paper on pages 102 to 107, which illustrates a variety of ways to incorporate quotations into your text. Note the punctuation also.

As you are writing, check carefully to see whether

a. you are not merely "stringing quotes" together without enough of your own wording;

b. you have already put a check mark on the notecard to show that you have previously used that material;

c. you have introduced each quoted passage with an appropriate transition;

d. you have analyzed your source material to make it work for you in your paper by showing your reader specifically how it applies to your argument. Don't just cite a quotation and run off. You have just stated that someone said something; now answer the question, "So what?" Why are you telling this to your reader?

8. Even before you finish the first writing (rough draft), you may want to rearrange some material already written. If so, see the first paragraph under STEP 8; the directions there will facilitate your work if you decide to insert or change material as you write.

9. When you have taken information from a notecard, whether it is a directly quoted passage or not, stop where the passage ends. If you are using the parenthetical reference form of documentation (see STEP 9 pp. 81–83), insert the author and page number taken from your notecard, in parentheses, here. If you are using the footnote or endnote style (see STEP 9 pp. 83–85), draw cut-off lines across the page. Be sure to do this at the exact point where the material

---

Smith (71)

---

calls for documentation. Leave enough space so that you can fill in your full footnote or endnote later; right now, while your notecard is in your hand, simply put in the author's name (like Smith above) and the page number (like (71) above) from which the information came. It is essential to copy this information exactly. It is the only way that you can be assured that your documentation is accurate.

If your cut-off lines come in the middle of the sentence, continue after the cut-off lines as if they were not there. If you are using a computer, you may have a program that will insert the footnote for you at the bottom of the page. *See* "Using Footnotes or Endnotes" and "Procedure for Writing Footnotes or Endnotes" and "Footnote Forms" in STEP 9. Put a check mark in the bottom left corner of a notecard once you have used the information on it so that you will be sure not to use the same material again.

10. Develop each section of your outline considering each as a separate essay for the time being. Just as you could not expect to write five essays in one day, so you cannot hope to develop more than one section of a long paper at a time.

11. Remember to revise your outline if you make any changes as you write your first draft. By the time you complete your first draft your outline will be the blueprint of your actual paper.

12. Be sure to number pages of your first draft or have the computer do it for you automatically. If you are typing your paper and need to add pages, simply number the inserted pages also; for example, if they come after page 8, number the inserted pages 8A, 8B, and so on.

CHECK LIST FOR FREQUENT ERRORS IN WRITING THE RESEARCH PAPER

When you have finished your first draft, it is important to look over your writing, checking particularly for basic errors that frequently appear on the final draft. It is a good idea for you to find them yourself before handing in a paper; if you don't, your instructor will. Of course all the rules of good writing—including grammatical structure, coherence, unity, good paragraphing, correct spelling, and accurate choice of words—apply, but the items on the list of errors that follows are frequently corrected on student research papers:

1. Your sources are not integrated. You use all material from one source and then all from another; your reader could just pick up one book and read certain pages and then the next one. Real research involves the blending together of ideas from many different sources. (*See* p. 77.)

2. using Latin (i.e., *ibid.*) in in-text or footnote reference. (*See* p. 93.)

3. not blocking a long quotation properly. (*See* p. 97.)

4. using phrases that are too similar to the words of your source and that would be considered plagiarized. (*See* pp. 120–127.)

5. moving from one idea to another without transitions that indicate to the reader what the relationship is between the two ideas. Use transitional phrases such as "as a result," "consequently," "another less important reason," and "on the other hand." (*See* pp. 73 and 76.)

6. introducing punctuation errors, especially the use of quotation marks. (*See* p. 63.)

7. using a quotation without analyzing it and leaving it up to the reader to decide how it fits into your argument and/or how you are interpreting it for that purpose. (*See* p. 72.)

8. using the passive voice, such as "it was decided by Professor Jones that such and such is true." Change to "Professor Jones decided that such and such is true."

9. numbering pages incorrectly. Any page with a title should have a number at bottom and the rest should be numbered carefully on top. (*See* p. 96.)

10. not showing source of information; all information from sources *must* be documented. (*See* pp. 79–80 and 120–127.)

11. using incorrect footnote form. (*See* pp. 84–94.)

12. using incorrect bibliographical form. (*See* pp. 25–42.)

13. using obsolete publications for a current subject, such as for information about computers, the treatment of disease, divorce laws, or other subjects that change radically and quickly.

14. using sources that are not reliable and whose information is not documented. (*See* p. 15.)

STEP

REVISE THE TEXT; WRITE INTRODUCTION AND CONCLUSION

The best way to revise your work is to read the paper aloud after a waiting period. If you are not using a word processor that moves your material around for you, avoid the necessity of recopying your work by using scissors to cut out material that belongs elsewhere. Be sure to cut out, or move in your word processor, any documentation that belongs with the passage you are moving. Simply tape the whole insert where it belongs; you may need to cut that page in order to insert the interpolated material. It is essential that you keep the foot-note or parenthetical reference with the material it documents. Accuracy in this regard is crucial. Computer bibliographical programs will do this for you when you move text, but be very careful if you are moving text on your own.

1. Check to see that you have followed the basic rules for good English sentence structure and style.

2. Check to see that you have followed the principles of rhetoric in your sentence structure, paragraph development, and diction.

3. Check to see that you have smooth transitions (connections) from sentence to sentence, paragraph to paragraph, and section to section. Check particularly to see that the quoted material is

integrated into the text so that, together with your writing, it presents a unified piece of work. Check also the punctuation before and after the quoted material used as part of your own sentence; a good test is to ask yourself whether you would use a comma, a colon, or other punctuation if there were no quotation marks within that sentence. (See Card G, page 61.) When you hear a well-prepared lecture, you are not aware that the lecturer has gathered material from many different sources, part of which he or she is quoting directly and some of which is being paraphrased. You should give the same impression to your reader. Often the addition of a few connecting words will result in smooth transitions.

4. Check to see that your finished paper sounds logically developed and that everything that you have included in your paper presents relevant, logical proof of your thesis. Draw a line through anything that does not, and eliminate it now.

5. Check to see that you have avoided the repetition of facts or ideas. A "padded" paper is boring and meaningless.

6. Be sure that specific examples are provided for all general statements whether they are from other sources or your own. Most ideas need to be explained and/or illustrated in order to be clear.

WRITE THE INTRODUCTION

Now that you know exactly what you are about to introduce, you can write an introductory section to your paper. You can use your introduction to do the following:

1. point out the timeliness or value of your research;

2. define an abstract or special term used in your thesis;

3. explain why you have taken this particular aspect of your topic;

4. inform your reader of the various aspects of your topic other than the one you have chosen;

5. give a pertinent anecdote that provides a direct means of leading into your topic;

6. summarize how you have approached your topic.

Whatever your approach, your introduction should be relevant; it should gain the immediate attention of your reader, and it should clarify your thesis in some way.

WRITE THE CONCLUSION

The conclusion of the research paper is the most valuable single part of it. All the material you have gathered means nothing to your reader until you present the conclusion you have reached as a result of your research. Restate your thesis and show what the material you have presented adds up to. Analyze and evaluate your main points for your reader; also consider the ramifications and general implications of them to your conclusion. Although no actual new information is usually introduced in the concluding paragraphs, the conclusion is the only "original" contribution you offer in your paper. It manifests the value of your research as well as your understanding of the material that you have presented. It should be a strong recapitulation of your major ideas.

Now read the entire paper aloud again and listen to how it sounds before you fill in the footnotes. It should flow smoothly throughout; supply transitions wherever you sense a lack of continuity from one idea to the next.

STEP

FILL IN PARENTHETICAL REFERENCES OR FOOTNOTES ON DRAFT

All information taken from the work of others needs to be documented. Normally, every paragraph except those that develop your own completely original ideas will have at least one parenthetical reference or footnote.

WHAT TO DOCUMENT

All important statements of fact and all opinions, whether directly quoted or paraphrased, and all paraphrases of those facts that are not common knowledge should be documented by a footnote or parenthetical reference to the exact page in the source where you found your information. If you are not quoting printed matter, your parenthetical reference or footnote should tell the reader where and how you found out the particular material you need to document.

WHAT NOT TO DOCUMENT

1. Well-known, generally accepted facts need not be documented unless you want to document someone's questioning or analysis of those facts.

2. Any material that comes from commonly recognized sources or quotations need not be documented; you may say that all men are created equal or that all the world's a stage or that the heavens declare the glory of God without referring in context or footnote to the Declaration of Independence, to Shakespeare, or to the Bible, respectively.

STYLES OF DOCUMENTATION

Documentation is properly placed as parenthetical references (notes that appear in the text itself), footnotes (notes that appear at the bottom of the page), or as endnotes (notes that appear at the end of a chapter or short paper). The form for footnotes and endnotes is identical. However, in order to avoid confusion, such notes will be generally referred to here as either *notes* or *footnotes*, but it should be understood that these notes may be placed either at the bottom of the page or at the end of a chapter or paper. Common usage supports the term *footnotes* for all note documentation, even though the notes are placed entirely at the end of the paper as endnotes rather than at the bottom of a page where they would properly be called *footnotes*.

OTHER USES OF PARENTHETICAL REFERENCES AND FOOTNOTES

1. Definitions that would interrupt the text but might be helpful to the reader should be in a footnote. (*See* footnote 3 of Sample Paper 1 (p. 107) and footnote 27 of Sample Paper 2 (p. 115).)

2. Material that would detract from the focus of your paper but which would supply valuable and enriching information to the reader should be in a footnote, not in the text of your paper. This material may be in your own words or in words you quote from an authority. Also, the footnote may simply refer the reader to another source or sources where a fuller discussion may be

found. (*See* footnotes 1 and 5 of Sample Paper 1 (p. 107) and footnotes 5 and 36 of Sample Paper 2 (pp. 113 and 115).)

3. Cross-references to other parts of your own paper may be made in parenthetical references or footnotes. (*See* footnote 4 of Sample Paper 1 (p. 107) and footnote 29 of Sample Paper 2 (p. 115).)

USING PARENTHETICAL REFERENCES

Parenthetical references are much simpler than footnotes or endnotes. The MLA style of reference requires that documentation be inserted within the text of your writing as brief parenthetical references to the relevant bibliography entries. These references basically provide the author's last name and a page number to identify the source and the specific location within it from which your material came. Further information regarding the source can be found in the list of works cited in the bibliography of your paper. Therefore the information in the parenthetical reference must match the corresponding information in the bibliography. Sample Paper 1 (pp. 102–107) is documented in this fashion.

PROCEDURE FOR WRITING PARENTHETICAL REFERENCES

1. Take out the bibliography card from which your material came.

2. Place the reference as close as possible to the material it documents, but only where a pause would naturally occur, such as at the end of a sentence. The parenthetical acknowledgment precedes the punctuation mark that concludes the sentence, clause, or phrase containing the material you have borrowed. If the quotation comes at the end of the sentence, the parenthetical reference should be enclosed after the closing quotation mark and before the concluding punctuation mark.

3. Within the parentheses there is no punctuation between the author's name and the page number if the volume number or other information is given. The abbreviation for page is never used, and there is never any end punctuation within the parentheses.

4. Copy the page number on which the material was found exactly as you have it on your notecard; if the source is a multivolume work, the volume number appears after the author's name followed by a colon and the page number. If a pamphlet or booklet has no page number, supply a page number in brackets or write the words *no page*.

5. Take out the bibliography card to make sure that you have copied the author's name exactly. Draw a check mark on the card to remind yourself that you have used that source and that it must be included in your final bibliography.

FORMS FOR PARENTHETICAL REFERENCES

1. If the work to be cited was written by a single author and is alphabetized in the bibliography under the author's last name, your parenthetical reference will give the author's last name followed by a page number: (Campbell 37).

2. If you have already given the author's name in your text in connection with this material, then you would give only the page number in the reference: (37). In the case of multiple authors of a single work or a corporate author with a long name, it is preferable to mention the name or names in the text, leaving just the page number for the parenthetical reference, rather than having a long, unwieldy parenthetical reference that would interrupt the flow of your writing.

3. If there is no author, that is, if your bibliographical entry begins with a title, use the title or the first word under which it is alphabetized if it is long: (*Máscaras* 26).

4. If there are two authors, use both last names: (Markman and Markman 123). 1f there are three, use all three (Broda, Carrasco, and Matos Moctezuma ix). If there are more than three, use the first author's last name followed by "and others": (Lothrop and others 87).

5. If there is no author, but the bibliographical entry begins with the name of an editor, a translator, or a compiler, use the last name of that person followed by the page number: (Apostolos-Cappadona 86).

6. If the author is a corporate entity, or if the work cited is a government document, use the name of the originating entity or the first word under which it is alphabetized: (Instituto Guerrerense de la Cultura 21) or (Instituto 21).

7. If your reference is to one volume in a multi-volume set, give the author's last name followed by the volume number, a colon, and the page number: (Budge 2:23).

   In the case of nonprint media (records, films, television and radio shows, etc.) there will, of course, be no page number: (Brahms).

8. If the bibliography contains only one work by the author cited, you should give only the author's last name to identify the work unless, of course, there were two authors with the same last name in which case you would have to give the first name too.

9. If there is more than one book by the author in the bibliography, give the title or an abbreviated form of it after the author's name.

10. If you include an author's name in the sentence, you should omit it from the parenthetical reference that follows; you need only give the page number.

   Remember that the point of your documentation is to direct the reader to the correct source in your bibliography where the rest of the information can be found and to give the precise page, volume of a multivolume work, or the act, scene, and line of a play from which the material came in that source. References should be kept as brief as possible as long as the accuracy of locating the material is assured.

   Footnotes should still be used for material that would disrupt the flow of the text, such as definitions, explanations, and cross-references. (*See* items 1, 2, and 3 in section "Other Uses of Parenthetical References and Footnotes," pp. 80–81.) Also if you need to refer to several sources for an acknowledgment, it is best to cite them in a footnote.

USING FOOTNOTES OR ENDNOTES

Decide where you are going to put your documentation; there are two acceptable places. Endnotes are placed after the text of the research paper or chapter. Start them on a new page entitled ENDNOTES numbered in sequence with the preceding page. Footnotes, on the other hand, are placed at the bottom of the page on which the foot-note number occurred in the text. The first footnote begins four lines (two double spaces) after the last line of the text. You can make a line on the third line above by striking the underline key fifteen times and then double space before writing the footnote number. Endnotes are generally simpler and preferable unless you are instructed otherwise, or unless you are using a computer program that will do the spacing, numbering, and form for your footnotes and/or your endnotes.

PROCEDURE FOR WRITING FOOTNOTES OR ENDNOTES

1. Take out the bibliography card from which your material came.

2. Write your footnote or endnote as you would a sentence; do not separate into lines as you did on the bibliography card.

3. Write the number of the note in either of two ways, but be con-sistent:

   a. above the line as it must be in the text or

   b. on the same line as the note will be.

   For the former, use no period after the number; for the latter, be sure to use a period and two spaces before beginning your note. Check to see that the number in the text matches the number given for the note. Remember that notes are numbered consec-utively throughout the paper; there will be only one note num-bered 1 in any short paper (fewer than fifty typewritten pages) or for each chapter in a long paper.

4. Indent the note number and first line as for a paragraph; bring the second and each succeeding line of the same note back to the margin of the text.

5. Fill in all information from the bibliography card exactly as it is written with these exceptions:

   a. write the author's name in regular order (not reversed) fol-lowed by a comma, not a period;

   b. omit the period after the name of a book; put a comma instead of a period after the name of an article;

    c. enclose within parentheses the publication facts for a book (city, publisher, date), omitting the period after the date.

  6. Copy exactly the page number from which the material came. If a pamphlet or booklet has no page number, supply a page number in brackets or write the words *no page* after the comma.

  7. Put a period at the end of the note.

  8. Before you put your bibliography card away, put a check mark on the bottom left corner to remind yourself that you have used this source once for a first-entry footnote and that it must be included in your final bibliography.

  9. All future references to this source or to any other source already documented in full will be in second-entry footnote form. *See* pp. 93–94.

FOOTNOTE FORMS

The following examples show the footnote form for each of the bibliography cards and entries used in STEP 4, pages 25–42.

FORMS FOR FIRST ENTRY FOOTNOTES
From a Source that Is Not Part of a Larger Work

NOTE: When typing your own footnotes remember that you will underline all items that appear in italics. Of course, if you are using a computer, you will use the *italics* font.

      Some writers do not include in footnotes all of the publication data if a bibliography is given at the end of the paper; however, many colleges do require the following full form as well as a bibliography.

1. the basic form

[1]Joseph Campbell, *The Inner Reaches of Outer Space: Metaphor as Myth and as Religion* (New York: Alfred van der Marck Editions, 1986) 28.

2. no author

[2]*Máscaras Mexicanas: de la Colección del Ing. Victor José Moya* (México: Dirección de Museos del Instituto Nacional de Antropología e Historia, 1974) 97–99.

3. two authors

[3]Roberta H. Markman and Peter T. Markman, *The Flayed God: The Mesoamerican Mythological Tradition* (San Francisco: Harper San Francisco, 1992) 36.

4. three authors

[4]Johanna Broda, Davíd Carrasco, and Eduardo Matos Moctezuma, *The Great Temple of Tenochtitlan: Center and Periphery in the Aztec World* (Berkeley: University of California Press, 1987) 112.

5. more than three authors

[5]Samuel K. Lothrop and others, *Essays in Pre-Columbian Art and Archaeology* (Cambridge, Massachusetts: Harvard University Press, 1961) 47.

6. corporate authorship

[6]Instituto Guerrerense de la Cultura, *Calendario de Fiestas del Estado de Guerrero* (Chilpancingo, Guerrero, México: Instituto Guerrerense de la Cultura, 1987) 22.

7. an author and an editor

[7]Joseph Campbell, *The Power of Myth* with Bill Moyers, ed. Betty Sue Flowers (New York: Doubleday, 1988) 78–79.

8. an author and a translator

[8]Mircea Eliade, *Images and Symbols*, trans. Philip Mairet (Kansas City, Missouri: Sheed Andrews and McMeel, 1961) 152.

9. an author, an editor, and a translator

[9]Pablo Neruda, *A New Decade (Poems: 1958–1967)*, ed. Ben Belitt, trans. Ben Belitt and Alastair Reid (New York: Grove Press, 1969) 105.

10. an editor but no author

[10]Diane Apostolos-Cappadona, ed., *Symbolism, the Sacred, and the Arts* (New York: Crossroad, 1988) ix.

NOTE: This form would be used to refer to a section of the anthology other than one of the individually titled pieces as well as for any other book with an editor but no author; for a reference to an essay in this anthology, see example 32 following.

11. a translator and an editor but no author

[11]Thelma D. Sullivan, trans., *A Scattering of Jades: Stories, Poems, and Prayers of the Aztecs*, ed. T. J. Knab (New York: Simon and Schuster, 1994) 68.

12. a compiler

[12]Curt Muser, comp., *Facts and Artifacts of Ancient Middle America* (New York: E. P. Dutton, 1978) 44.

13. one volume in a multivolume set when all volumes have the same title

[13]E. A. Wallis Budge, *The Gods of the Egyptians or Studies in Egyptian Mythology* (1904; rpt. New York: Dover Publications, 1969) 2:361.

NOTE: The volume number, 2, appears before the colon and the page number, 361, appears after.
  This book is a modern reprint of an older edition; see example 18.

14. one volume in a multivolume set when each volume has a separate title

[14]Michael D. Coe and Richard A. Diehl, *The People of the River*, vol. 2 of *In the Land of the Olmec* (Austin: University of Texas Press, 1980) 119.

15. a book in a series edited by one other than the author

[15]David Maclagen, *Creation Myths: Man's Introduction to the World*, in the *Art and Imagination* series, ed. Jill Purce (London: Thames and Hudson, 1977) 112–115.

16. a book with a subtitle or secondary title

[16]Vincent F. Hopper ed. and trans. *Chaucer's Canterbury Tales: An Interlinear Translation* (Woodbury, New York: Barron's 1970) 17.

NOTE: Obviously Chaucer did not write a book with this title; therefore this entry is correct for this book. However, if you quoted
the lines from Chaucer with the older spelling, your footnote
would be thus:
[16]Geoffrey Chaucer, "The Pardoner's Tale," *Chaucer's Canterbury Tales: An Interlinear Translation*, ed. and trans. Vincent F. Hopper (Woodbury, New York: Barron's, 1970) 299.

17. an edition subsequent to the first edition

[17]Michael D. Coe, *The Maya*, 5th ed. (New York: Thames and
Hudson, 1993) 29.

18. a modern reprint of an older edition

[18]Frances Toor, *Mexican Popular Arts* (1939; rpt. Detroit:
Blaine Ethridge Books, 1973) 106.

19. a pamphlet, bulletin, manual, or monograph

[19]Lenore H. Mulryan, *Mexican Figural Ceramists and Their
Work*, Monograph Series, no. 16 (Los Angeles: Museum of Cultural
History, University of California, Los Angeles, 1982) 16.

20. a catalog of an exhibition

[20]Erika Billeter, ed., *The Blue House: The World of Frida
Kahlo,* an exhibit at the Schirn Kunsthalle, Frankfurt, March 6–May
23, 1993 and The Museum of Fine Arts, Houston, June 6–August 29,
1993 (Frankfurt: Schirn Kunsthalle and Houston: Museum of Fine
Arts, 1993) 11.

21. a government document

[21]U.S. Congressional Record, 80th Cong., 2nd Sess., 1948,
XCII, Part 6, 5539.

22. a dictionary

[22]*Webster's New Collegiate Dictionary* (Springfield, Massachusetts: G. & C. Merriam Company, 1984).

NOTE: No page number is required since the dictionary is arranged
alphabetically.

23. a record, audiotape, or compact disc

[23]Johannes Brahms, *Violin Sonatas Nos. 1–3*, Itzhak Perlman, violin and Vladimir Ashkenazy, piano, EMI/Angel, CDC 7 47403 2. Compact disc.

24. a film or videotape

[24]*Wings of Desire*, Wim Wenders, Director (Orion Pictures, 1988).

25. a radio program

[25]*Tribute: Ernest von Dohnanyi*, KFAC (1330 AM, 92.3 FM), Los Angeles, 7–8 p.m., 26 July 1988.

26. a television program

[26]Moyers: *Joseph Campbell and the Power of Myth*, pt. 1, KCET (Channel 28), Los Angeles, PBS, 10–11 p.m., 23 May 1988.

From a Source Contained Within a Larger Work

27. the basic form

[27]Gregory S. Jay, "Knowledge, Power, and the Struggle for Representation," *College English* January 1994: 12.

28. a periodical article with no author

[28]"The Presidential Policy Scoreboard," *The World and I* June 1988: 52–55.

29. a titled book review

[29]Octavio Paz, "Food of the Gods," trans. Eliot Weinberger, review of *The Blood of Kings* by Linda Schele and Mary Ellen Miller, *The New York Review of Books* 26 February 1987: 3–7.

30. an untitled book review

[30]Franke J. Neumann, review of *Masks of the Spirit: Image and Metaphor in Mesoamerica* by Peter T. Markman and Roberta H. Markman, *Religious Studies Review* April 1993: 179.

31. a newspaper article or editorial

[31]Dan Williams, "400-Year Church Ties Cut by Ancient Mexican Tribe," *Los Angeles Times* 5 July 1987: I:1.

NOTE: For an unsigned article, you would begin with the title of the article. I:1 indicates that the information to which you are referring is on page 1 of section I.

32. an essay (or other work) written by one person in an anthology edited by another

[32]Mircea Eliade, "The Symbolism of Shadows in Archaic Religions," *Symbolism, the Sacred, and the Arts,* ed. Diane Apostolos-Cappadona (New York: Crossroads, 1988) 5.

33. an encyclopedia article

[33]Kees W. Bolle, "Myth and Mythology: The Nature, Functions, and Types of Myth," *The New Encyclopaedia Britannica: Macropaedia,* 15th ed., 1986, 24:713.

NOTE: For an unsigned article, you would begin with the title of the article. Remember that most articles are signed with intials only; you must look at the beginning of the first volume to find the author's full name.

34. an introduction or limited part of a book by one other than the author

[34]Joseph Campbell, "Introduction," *Masks of the Spirit: Image and Metaphor in Mesoamerica,* Peter T. Markman and Roberta H. Markman (Berkeley: University of California Press, 1989) xv.

35. author of a work in a book in a series edited by others

[35]Jack Waardenburg, "Symbolic Aspects of Myth," *Myth, Symbol, and Reality,* ed. Alan M. Olson, vol. 1 of The Boston University Studies in Philosophy and Religion, ed. Leroy S. Rouner (Notre Dame, Indiana: University of Notre Dame Press, 1980) 53.

36. a reprint with critical comment by the editor

[36]Andrew Wright, "Afterword," Joyce Cary, *The Horse's Mouth* (1944; rtp. New York: Harper & Row/Perennial Library, 1965) 349.

37. a casebook (a text for controlled research)

[37]David Stevenson, "J. D. Salinger: The Mirror of Crisis," *The Nation*, 9 March 1957: 215; rpt. *If You Really Want to Know: A Catcher Casebook*, ed. Malcolm M. Marsden (Chicago: Scott, Foresman, 1963) 22.

NOTE: There are two ways to use a casebook: as an anthology of essays about a particular subject or as a library containing essays, which you will read and document as if you were reading the original. For the latter use, the original pagination appears in the casebook with slash marks wherever a page change occurred in the original. Check with your instructor about how to use the casebook, but it would never be wrong to use this model form.

From Other Types of Sources

38. an interview

[38]Roberta H. Markman, Professor of Comparative Literature, California State University, Long Beach, personal interview on Mexican masks, Long Beach, California, 16 April 1994.

NOTE: Unless the person interviewed is well known, you should indicate through the use of the person's title why he or she is an authority on the subject of the interview.

39. an unpublished lecture

[39]Peter T. Markman, Professor of English, Fullerton College, class lecture on Carlos Fuentes, *The Death of Artemio Cruz*, Fullerton College, Fullerton, California, 3 May 1992.

40. a published lecture

[40]Kurt Vonnegut, Jr., "Address to Graduating Class at Bennington College, 1970," *Wampeters, Foma and Granfalloons (Opinions)* (New York: Dell, 1976) 163.

41. mimeographed or photocopied material

[41]Betty Ann Brown, "Fiestas de Oaxaca," 1977 (mimeographed) 3.

42. an unpublished thesis or dissertation

[42]Roberta H. Markman, "Mann's Joseph: From Dreamer to Artist," diss., Occidental College, Los Angeles, 1969, 308.

43. a letter

[43]Unpublished letter from Ernest Hemingway to Roberta Hoffman, dated August 12, 1957.

44. The Bible or any well-known literary work that can be identified by book or scene plus lines or by chapter and verse

[44]I Corinthians 13:12, The Bible, Revised Standard Version.

NOTE: The names of sacred scripture are neither underlined nor put in quotation marks. The translation of the Bible is assumed to be the King James Version unless another is named, as in the preceding example.

[44]John Milton, *Paradise Lost*, bk. I, II. 13–14.

NOTE: The particular edition you used is not needed unless the work is a translation.

The name of a novel, play, or long poem would be underlined even if it is part of an anthology.

45. an abridgment

[45]*Style Manual* (abridged), rev. ed. (Washington, D.C.: Government Printing Office, 1984) 19.

46. record jacket notes

[46]Gustav Mahler, *Symphony No. 4*, Concertgebouw Orchestra, Amsterdam, cond. Bernard Haitink (Philips, SAL 3729 802 888 LY), jacket notes.

47. a pamphlet included with a record

[47]Richard Kostelanetz and Editors of Time-Life Records, "A Listener's Guide to the Recordings," *The Music of Today* in *The Story of Great Music* series (Time-Life Records, STL 145) 3.

48. a lecture on a record or tape

[48]Thomas Sherman, narrator and conductor, "Musical Program Notes," Bethoven's *Symphony No. 5 in C Minor, Op. 67*, Sir Adrian Boult conducting The Philharmonic Promenade Orchestra of London (Vanguard, MARS 3005).

49. computer software

[49]John A. Weyh, Joseph R. Crook, and Les N. Hauge, *The Mole Concept*, pt. 2 of *Concepts in General Chemistry*, computer software, COMPress, IBM PC.

50. a computer database

[50]Thomas Sanchez, "The Rituals of the Maya," *American Journal of Anthropology* 1993, Dialog file 10, item 976–977: 12.

ABBREVIATED FORMS FOR SECOND-ENTRY FOOTNOTES

For every first-entry footnote (the first time you document information from a source) you will give the complete bibliographical information *plus* the exact page number, which you have already entered in the cutoff lines. See STEP 7, p. 73. For all succeeding footnotes referring to that source, use the second-entry form.

1. Current usage has eliminated Latin from footnotes. (*See* section of abbreviations on pp. 146–148 so that you will know what the Latin terms indicate when you see them used in older texts.) Current form now requires that for second-entry footnotes you give only enough to identify the source such as the author's name and page number:

   Campbell 20–21.

2. If two or more works by the same author have been used, such as Campbell's *The Power of Myth* and his *The Inner Reaches of Outer Space: Metaphor as Myth and as Religion*, a shortened form of the title should follow the author's last name for all second-entry footnotes, such as Campbell, Power 31.

   Campbell, Inner 20–21.

3. If two or more authors with the same last name have been used, the first name should be given, and if either one has two or more works cited in the paper, a short title must be given for each:

> Joseph Campbell, <u>Inner</u> 48.
>
> Joseph Campbell, <u>Power</u> 20–21.
>
> Jack R. Campbell 42–46.

4. If you have a footnote referring to a source without an author:

> "The Presidential Policy Scoreboard" 53.

A title may be shortened by using an ellipsis:

> "The Presidential . . ." 53.

5. If reference information is given in the text, the second-entry footnote may simply include the information that is missing, such as the page number (if the author has been mentioned in connection with the information) or the title and page if there is more than one work by the author cited in the paper. However, it is not incorrect to repeat the author's name or the text in the note.

STEP

PUT THE PAPER IN FINAL FORM

THE ELEMENTS

1. Format

If possible, a research paper should be typewritten on regular (never thin) paper and double-spaced except for blocked quotations, footnotes, and bibliography; otherwise, it should be written in blue or black ink as neatly and legibly as possible. Leave good margins on all four sides of the paper, allowing sufficient extra room on the left side for binding. The finished paper should be fastened with a title page. If your instructor prefers, the paper should be bound in a folder with the title, your name, the course number, and the date on the outside.

2. Title Page

Include a title page on which you state the title of the paper, your name, the course (and section number, if any) for which the paper was written, the name of the institution (often considered optional), and the date the paper is submitted.

3. Preface

The dedication on the preface page, if there is one, is inserted after the title page; it is not numbered. The title of the page,

DEDICATION or PREFACE, is centered and typed with capital letters.

4. Outline

The outline page serves as a table of contents, although it is not necessary to show page numbers for the short paper. The title of the page, OUTLINE, is centered and typed in capital letters. The page is numbered, and since the first page of your outline is a title page, the number is centered at the bottom of the page and is given in Roman numerals (lowercase) because nothing is numbered in Arabic numerals until the first page of the text.

After the title, OUTLINE, skip two lines and state the thesis sentence (after the word Thesis:). Follow that statement with the outline proper.

5. First Page of Text

The title of your paper is centered horizontally on the first (and no other) page of the text and typed in capital letters.

6. Documentation

The references will be written exactly as you have filled them in on the rough draft of your paper. For detailed information concerning documentation forms on the final copy, see STEP 9.

7. Pagination

Every page that is a title page (i.e., the first page of the outline, of the endnotes, and of the bibliography; the dedication page; the preface; and so forth) is numbered at the bottom center of that title page. The number is written usually without punctuation. All other pages of the paper are numbered in the upper right-hand corner of the page; the number is written alone or followed by a period. The pages are numbered consecutively from the first page of the text to the last page of the bibliography.

8. Quotations

Short quotations: Quoted short passages and/or sentences are woven into the text of your paragraph and should blend smoothly with your own style and the tense you are using. In the sample research paper on pages 102–107, you will see many examples of quotations (and paraphrases) woven into the text and made meaningful by the context in which they appear. Notice that before and after each quoted passage the punctuation is determined by what is needed to make the passage fit smoothly into the sentence. In other words, the test for punctuating before or after a quoted passage is this: Would you need a mark of punctuation at that point in your sentence if there were no quotation marks?

Longer (blocked) quotations: Sometimes, as in the sample papers, pp. 102 and 104, a quoted passage is too long to be woven into your own sentence; it is an entity in itself and must be set off from the paragraph in which it appears. In fact, any directly quoted material that is longer than three lines must be blocked and single-spaced.

To set off a blocked passage: Double space before the quote. Indent the entire passage seven spaces from the left margin. If a new paragraph begins in the blocked passage, indicate that by indenting three additional spaces. Stop three spaces before the right-hand margin begins. Single space each line of the quoted passage, and then double space before the text of your paper continues. If the quoted and blocked passage is longer than one paragraph, double space between paragraphs within the same blocked passage. Do not use quotation marks at the beginning or end since the single spacing is a substitute for them. However, you would use double or single quotation marks even in a blocked passage to enclose any material that is in double or single quotation marks in the source you are citing. In other words, a blocked quoted passage looks exactly as it did in the source you used.

Footnote number: The footnote number is put above the line and after the closing quotation mark or after the last word in a blocked passage.

9. Bibliography

The bibliography is always the last section of a research paper. (*See* STEP 4 for final bibliography forms.)

10. Final Step

Proofread your paper carefully for typographical errors.

A SAMPLE RESEARCH PAPER

Two copies of the research paper itself (excluding cover page, outline, and bibliography) have been included. This will demonstrate the forms used for both the newer parenthetical type of documentation and the paper documented entirely with endnotes or footnotes. Each form has been described in detail in STEP 9. The bibliography would be the same in either case.

NOTE: Since it is neither expedient nor necessary to reproduce an entire paper for the sake of illustrating the techniques explained in this manual, the pages that follow contain a full sentence outline and only that part of the paper that expands the thesis. (Normally, the first part of any research paper, the introduction, develops the thesis and clarifies the point of view from which the writer has limited his or her paper.) Also included is a bibliography listing only the sources used in this introductory section of the longer paper by Markman, from which this introductory section is taken. Normally, a short research paper such as this one would not have as many footnotes or as much quoted material; however, it is important for the student to see how a wide variety of material could be used and documented.

WORDS AND PICTURES:
THE MYTHIC VISION IN TALES AND ART

by

Roberta H. Markman

Comparative Literature 452, Section I
California State University, Long Beach
January 3, 1994

OUTLINE

Thesis: Humanity's attempt to understand the basic phenomena of life is expressed metaphorically both verbally in mythology and visually in mythic art.

I. The process of creation is expressed metaphorically in both mythology and art.

A. Both mythology and art express the concept of genesis through the metaphoric image of the joining of opposites.

1. Sometimes the primordial couple (the joining of masculine and feminine) provides the metaphor in both mythology and art.

2. Sometimes the integration of light and dark is the metaphoric image for the creative process in both mythology and art.

3. Sometimes the weaving of warp and woof (vertical and horizontal) serves as the imagery for creation.

B. Both mythology and art express the concept of creation through the metaphor of the sun's pattern of dying and rising.

C. Both mythology and art show "the beginning" through the imagery of order emerging from chaos.

D. Both mythology and art express the creative process as the splitting of the whole, or single image, into two or more of its parts.

i

II. Humanity's relationship to the uni-
verse is expressed metaphorically in
both mythology and art.

A. Both mythology and art describe
various aspects of nature in their
relationship to the individual to
show the complex relationship of
the individual to the universal.

B. Both mythology and art use the
imagery of the human being and
God(s) to express and understand
the relationship of the unique to
the general.

III. The conception of death and an afterlife are metaphorically expressed in
both mythology and art in an attempt
to come to terms with these mysteries.

A. The phenomenon of a symbolic death
is expressed metaphorically in both
mythology and art.

1. The imagery of humanity's tran-
scendent temporal experience is
expressed metaphorically in both
mythology and art.

2. The imagery of the human being's
return from death, darkness, or
the underworld to a new life is
often the metaphor for the experience of death and resurrection.

B. Physical death and a spiritual
return, or transcendence, is shown
metaphorically in both mythology and
art.

SAMPLE PAPER 1
PARENTHETICAL REFERENCE STYLE

Note that endnotes are used within a paper using the parenthetical reference style to present information other than the reference. The endnotes included here represent a range of possibilities: an explanatory endnote (#1), the reference for a quotation documented in the work cited (# 2), a definition (#3), a cross-reference to your own paper (#4), and the notation of an additional source of information confirming, contradicting, or amplifying the source cited (#5).

WORDS AND PICTURES:
THE MYTHIC VISION IN TALES AND ART

Human beings everywhere have always been curious. They look around their world, poke and pry into its features, in order to understand everything that confronts them. We can see evidence of this even in the oldest stories that have come down to us. In the epic of <u>Gilgamesh</u>, from the second or third millennium B.C., for example, as in the later story of creation in Genesis, people were challenged to "name" the animals and the other features of their world. This "naming" is significant on many levels, but in its most symbolic sense it signifies their coming to understand the basic nature of things. In fact, the Biblical account of creation makes clear that the development of that understanding is God's intention in setting the task of naming (Genesis 1:26 and 2:19) and that the understanding involves an awareness of the relationship of what they have "named" to the "final, indivisible presence of Being itself" (Gingerich 109), that is, to God, thereby understanding it in the most fundamental sense.

As this suggests, human beings have always known that the world they inhabit consists of more than observable reality, and their curiosity has always extended beyond what they could see or touch. The same early stories show us that such aspects of life as creation and death, aspects that exist beyond the realms of intellect and logic, were similarly named

---

and thus understood. This "naming," however, has not always been verbal; the same need to understand is the most powerful impetus for the creation of visual art in traditional societies (Wingert 30), for such mythic art serves "to kindle into meaning [for human beings] aspects of their perception that would other- wise remain external to their minds" (Taylor 31). The ability to "name" what had been unknown provides the psychological security that human beings have always sought.

The curious individual, whether of one of today's technologically sophisticated, urban societies or of a "primal"[1] society of the present or distant past, begins this search for understanding with a question, and that question triggers the search that leads ultimately to an understanding that can be communi- cated through the fashioning of a mythic story or image (Eliade, Images 55-56). This is necessarily a process that begins in the individual since "the myths are metaphorical of spiritual potentiality in the [individual] human being, and the same powers that animate our life animate the life of the world" (Campbell, Power 22). The mythic images created as a result of the search express metaphorically the understanding that has been achieved, an understand- ing of the realm beyond the observable. Since myths and art use metaphors in that way to "speak about the unknowable in terms of the known" (Sproul 11), they are able to transmit the understanding of reality that results from the creative response to a confrontation with the unknown (Waardenburg 64).

Because they answer humanity's seemingly universal basic questions in particular ways, the myths define the cultures that create them (Watts xi), and, con- versely, they serve an important educational function in their community by expressing "the wisdom of life" as understood by that culture (Campbell Power 55). Pemberton illustrates this point in his discussion of the verses of the Odu recited by Ifa diviners of the African Yoruba culture. Through them he demonstrates that myth and art, by expressing the world view and values of their particular culture, explain the varying

roles of human beings and the powers that shape
their lives as well as help the Yoruba society
understand how to cope with its problems (66).
Because myths serve such functions as these, there
seems to be no question among scholars that myth is
essential to existence (Freund 233) or that "mere
purposive rationality," on the other hand, "unaided by
such phenomena as art, religion, dream...is necessarily pathogenic and destructive of life."[2]

Thus both mythology and mythic art create a kind
of cosmic order out of what appears to be chaos
(Segy 8), and by so doing are clearly not the <u>oppo-
site</u> of science (Sproul 16) or less valuable than
logic (Bolle 5). "Myths are fictional, to be sure,
but that fictional need not mean unreal and certainly
not unempirical" (Doty 4). The great myths, like
great art, are concerned with capturing the essence
of their subjects. Dorothy Jean Ray points this out
in her discussion of an Eskimo mask when she
explains how the image on the mask captures not an
individual animal, "but the vital force representing
a chain or continuum of all the individual spirits
of that genus which had lived, were living, or were
to live" (10). Its "truth," then, is not dependent on
reproducing the details of a particular visual reality. Going "beyond" the object in that way permits a
freedom from the limitations of the " 'historic
moment'" (Eliade, <u>Images</u> 13). It is in this sense
that "the artist penetrates—at times dangerously—into
the depths of the world and his own psyche" (Eliade
"The Sacred" 83), and it is for this reason and in
this way that "the artist...brings the images of a
mythology to manifestation; without images (whether
mental or visual) there is no mythology" (Campbell,
<u>Inner</u> 19).

These images may be expressed either in words or
graphically, and scholars have compared the verbally
expressed mythology and the visually expressed mythic
art of primal societies by considering their method-
ologies as well as their functions and thematic concerns. Human beings think in images and, according to
von Franz, "the only reality we can talk about...is

the _image_ of reality in our field of consciousness"
(11). Thus Jacques Waardenburg can say that a myth
"can be called a 'moving symbolism'" (54). Others
have also investigated this relationship. Cassirer
points out that "word magic is everywhere accompanied
by picture magic" (98), and Abel shows that both narrative myths and mythic art express a "common inner
source whose subject matter changes but whose nature
is the same" (41).

Ultimately, however, there is no doubt that

> the relationship between word and image is,
> potentially, at once metonymic[3] and meta-
> phoric: metonymic in that the two complete
> each other sequentially and as parts of a
> whole: metaphoric in that each translates
> into the other's medium. Ideally, image
> melts into speech, speech crystallizes the
> immediacy of the image (Gilman 63).

Thus it is primarily as metaphors that art and
mythology are able to serve as "poetic expressions
of...transcendental seeing."[4] By bringing together
"_two_ _frames_ _of_ _reference_ of which the reader [or
viewer] must be simultaneously aware" (Barbour 13),
both art and mythology "bring truth into being" (Segy
10) and serve the essential functions that have been
attributed to them. By juxtaposing everyday experiences to the images of imagination, the mundane is
metaphorically transformed into a revelation of the
" 'extraordinary' aspects of ordinary reality" (Waardenburg 43-44). As he wears a mask or plays out his
mythology in a ritual, "the man of the archaic societies becomes conscious of himself in an 'open world'
that is rich in meaning" (Eliade, _Images_ 178), detaching himself from his narrow environment (Foss 146).
It follows, then, that " 'to live' a symbol [in rit-
ual] and to decipher the messages [of ritual and
myth] correctly is equivalent to gaining access to
the universal" (Eliade, "The Symbolism" 13).

For traditional societies if the images created by
the visual and verbal arts are not "the vessels of
spiritual revelation," they fail as art and become

mere "things."[5] It is the very nature and power of
the metaphor that keep art and mythology from becoming "things." By creating and maintaining the tension
between the known and the unknown, the conscious and
the unconscious, the outer and the inner, the past
and the present, "the metaphor has the task of
destroying the rigid reduction and limitations of the
word" (Foss 120) and of bringing two images together
in a process that remains "eternally alive and universally accessible" (Eliade, Images 173); yet it
must, as David Attenborough says of a Dogon sculpture,
"be understood in its own terms" (140), as it would
have been by its creator. In myth "the word [or
image] speaks as if vested with its own authority"
(Veyne 110), for "myths convey what a culture has
chosen as its most important symbolic interpreta-
tions" (Doty 117).

Clearly then, "images, symbols and myths are not
irresponsible creations of the psyche; they respond
to a need and fulfill a function, that of bringing to
light the most hidden modalities of being" (Eliade,
Images 12). "Reaching into depths into which our
daily life with its various rituals can scarcely follow" (Foss 110), they capture the essence of the
human condition and force us to realize that the
human race cannot be divided into "primitives" and
moderns; there is a unity in the structure of humanity, and no one group can be considered inferior to
another (Bolle xiii). "The needs, aspirations, and
longings of mankind are similar" (Wingert 72), and as
we investigate the various manifestations of the
human attempt to understand the basic phenomena of
life through the metaphorical expression of insights,
both visually in art and verbally in mythology, we
will find that they speak to all people in "a language of vision which may tell us things about ourselves...that words alone cannot touch" (Mitchell
298-299). They will fulfill what Joseph Campbell
calls "the most essential service of a mythology,"
that "of opening the mind and heart to the utter
wonder of all being" (Inner 18).

ENDNOTES

[1]Following Jamake Highwater's suggestion (<u>The Primal Mind: Vision and Reality in Indian America</u> [New York: Harper & Row, 1981] xix), I will use <u>primal</u> instead of <u>primitive</u> when discussing technologically undeveloped traditional cultures to avoid the negative connotations of the latter term.

[2]Gregory Bateson, <u>Steps to an Ecology of Mind</u>; quoted in Bob Samples, <u>The Metaphoric Mind: A Celebration of Creative Consciousness</u> (Reading, Massachusetts: Addison-Wesley Publishing Co., Inc., 1976) ix.

[3]metonymic: using the name of one thing for that of another of which it is an attribute or with which it is associated.

[4]Campbell, <u>Myths</u> 31; specific illustrations of various metaphoric images and an explicit discussion of the ability of metaphor to transcend the mundane and profane by creatively expressing insights into the basic phenomena of life will be developed in the body of this paper; see outline on pages i-ii.

[5]Foss 111; see also <u>Máscaras</u> 15: "en muchas ocasiones la elaboracion de la mascara es parte del ritual y requiere que el individual este en un estado de pureza fisica y espiritual."

SAMPLE PAPER 2
ENDNOTE STYLE

Note that the references for this paper appear at the end of the paper as endnotes, but had they been placed at the bottom of each page as footnotes, the style and form for the references would be exactly the same.

WORDS AND PICTURES:
THE MYTHIC VISION IN TALES AND ART

Human beings everywhere have always been curious. They look around their world, poke and pry into its features, in order to understand everything that confronts them. We can see evidence of this even in the oldest stories that have come down to us. In the epic of Gilgamesh, from the second or third millennium B.C., for example, as in the later story of creation in Genesis, people were challenged to "name" the animals and the other features of their world. This "naming" is significant on many levels, but in its most symbolic sense it signifies their coming to understand the basic nature of things. In fact, the Biblical account of creation makes clear that the development of that understanding is God's intention in setting the task of naming[1] and that the understanding involves an awareness of the relationship of what they have "named" to the "final, indivisible presence of Being itself,"[2] that is, to God, thereby understanding it in the most fundamental sense.

As this suggests, human beings have always known that the world they inhabit consists of more than observable reality, and their curiosity has always extended beyond what they could see or touch. The same early stories show us that such aspects of life as creation and death, aspects that exist beyond the realms of intellect and logic, were similarly named and thus understood. This "naming," however, has not always been verbal; the same need to understand is the most powerful impetus for the creation of visual art in traditional societies,[3] for such mythic art serves "to kindle into meaning [for human beings] aspects of their perception that would otherwise remain external to their minds."[4] The ability to "name" what had been unknown provides the psychological security that human beings have always sought.

The curious individual, whether of one of today's technologically sophisticated, urban societies or of a "primal"[5] society of the present or distant past, begins this search for understanding with a question, and that question triggers the search that leads ultimately to an understanding that can be communicated through the fashioning of a mythic story or image.[6] This is necessarily a process that begins in the individual since "the myths are metaphorical of spiritual potentiality in the [individual] human being, and the same powers that animate our life animate the life of the world."[7] The mythic images created as a result of the search express metaphorically the understanding that has been achieved, an understanding of the realm beyond the observable. Since myths and art use metaphors in that way to "speak about the unknowable in terms of the known,"[8] they are able to transmit the understanding of reality that results from the creative response to a confrontation with the unknown.[9]

Because they answer humanity's seemingly universal basic questions in particular ways, the myths define the cultures that create them,[10] and, conversely, they serve an important educational function in their community by expressing "the wisdom of life" as understood by that culture.[11] Pemberton illustrates this point in his discussion of the verses of the Odu recited by Ifa diviners of the African Yoruba culture. Through them he demonstrates that myth and art, by expressing the world view and values of their particular culture, explain the varying roles of human beings and the powers that shape their lives as well as help the Yoruba society understand how to cope with its problems.[12] Because myths serve such functions as these, there seems to be no question among scholars that myth is essential to existence[13]

or that "mere purposive rationality," on the other
hand, "unaided by such phenomena as art, religion,
dream...is necessarily pathogenic and destructive of
life."[14]

Thus both mythology and mythic art create a kind
of cosmic order out of what appears to be chaos,[15] and
by so doing are clearly not the <u>opposite</u> of science[16]
or less valuable than logic.[17] "Myths are fictional,
to be sure, but that fictional need not mean unreal
and certainly not unempirical."[18] The great myths,
like great art, are concerned with capturing the
essence of their subjects. Dorothy Jean Ray points
this out in her discussion of an Eskimo mask when
she explains how the image on the mask captures
not an individual animal, "but the vital force representing a chain or continuum of all the individual
spirits of that genus which had lived, were living,
or were to live."[19] Its "truth," then, is not dependent on reproducing the details of a particular
visual reality. Going "beyond" the object in that
way permits a freedom from the limitations of the
"'historic moment.'"[20] It is in this sense that "the
artist penetrates—at times dangerously—into the
depths of the world and his own psyche,"[21] and it is
for this reason and in this way that "the artist...
brings the images of a mythology to manifestation;
without images (whether mental or visual) there is no
mythology."[22]

These images may be expressed either in words or
graphically, and scholars have compared the verbally
expressed mythology and the visually expressed mythic
art of primal societies by considering their method-
ologies as well as their functions and thematic concerns. Human beings think in images and, according to
von Franz, "the only reality we can talk about . . .
is the <u>image</u> of reality in our field of consciousness."[23] Thus Jacques Waardenburg can say that a myth
"can be called a 'moving symbolism.'"[24] Others have
also investigated this relationship. Cassirer points
out that "word magic is everywhere accompanied by
picture magic,"[25] and Abel shows that both narrative

myths and mythic art express a "common inner source whose subject matter changes but whose nature is the same."[26]

Ultimately, however, there is no doubt that.

> the relationship between word and image is, potentially, at once metonymic[27] and metaphoric: metonymic in that the two complete each other sequentially and as parts of a whole: metaphoric in that each translates into the other's medium. Ideally, image melts into speech, speech crystallizes the immediacy of the image.[28]

Thus it is primarily as metaphors that art and mythology are able to serve as "poetic expressions of...transcendental seeing."[29] By bringing together "two frames of reference of which the reader [or viewer] must be simultaneously aware,"[30] both art and mythology "bring truth into being"[31] and serve the essential functions that have been attributed to them. By juxtaposing everyday experiences to the images of imagination, the mundane is metaphorically transformed into a revelation of the "'extraordinary' aspects of ordinary reality."[32] As he wears a mask or plays out his mythology in a ritual, "the man of the archaic societies becomes conscious of himself in an 'open world' that is rich in meaning,"[33] detaching himself from his narrow environment.[34] It follows, then, that "'to live' a symbol [in ritual] and to decipher the messages [of ritual and myth] correctly is equivalent to gaining access to the universal."[35]

For traditional societies if the images created by the visual and verbal arts are not "the vessels of spiritual revelation," they fail as art and become mere "things."[36] It is the very nature and power of the metaphor that keep art and mythology from becoming "things." By creating and maintaining the tension between the known and the unknown, the conscious and the unconscious, the outer and the inner, the past and the present, "the metaphor has the task of destroying the rigid reduction and limitations of the

word"[37] and of bringing two images together in a
process that remains "eternally alive and universally
accessible";[38] yet it must, as David Attenborough says
of a Dogon sculpture, "be understood in its own
terms,"[39] as it would have been by its creator. In
myth "the word [or image] speaks as if vested with
its own authority,"[40] for "myths convey what a culture
has chosen as its most important symbolic interpreta-
tions."[41]

Clearly then, "images, symbols and myths are not
irresponsible creations of the psyche; they respond
to a need and fulfill a function, that of bringing to
light the most hidden modalities of being."[42] "Reaching into depths into which our daily life with its
various rituals can scarcely follow,"[43] they capture
the essence of the human condition and force us to
realize that the human race cannot be divided into
"primitives" and moderns; there is a unity in the
structure of humanity, and no one group can be considered inferior to another.[44] "The needs, aspirations,
and longings of mankind are similar,"[45] and as we
investigate the various manifestations of the human
attempt to understand the basic phenomena of life
through the metaphorical expression of insights, both
visually in art and verbally in mythology, we will
find that they speak to all people in "a language of
vision which may tell us things about
ourselves...that words alone cannot touch."[46] They
will fulfill what Joseph Campbell calls "the most
essential service of a mythology," that "of opening
the mind and heart to the utter wonder of all
being."[47]

ENDNOTES

[1]Genesis 1:26 and 2:19, The Bible, Revised Standard Version.

[2]Willard Gingerich, "Heidegger and the Aztecs: The Poetics of Knowing in Pre-Hispanic Nahuatl Poetry," Recovering the Word: Essays on Native American Literature, ed. Brian Swann and Arnold Krupat (Berkeley: University of California Press, 1987) 109.

[3]Paul S. Wingert, Primitive Art: Its Traditions and Styles (New York: New American Library, 1962) 30.

[4]Joshua C. Taylor, "Two Visual Excursions," The Language of Images, ed. W. J. T. Mitchell (Chicago: The University of Chicago Press, 1980) 31.

[5]Following Jamake Highwater's suggestion (The Primal Mind: Vision and Reality in Indian America [New York: Harper & Row, 1981] xix), I will use primal instead of primitive when discussing technologically undeveloped traditional cultures to avoid the negative connotations of the latter term.

[6]Mircea Eliade, Images and Symbols, trans. Philip Mairet (Kansas City, Missouri: Sheed Andrews and McMeel, 1961) 55-56.

[7]Joseph Campbell, The Power of Myth with Bill Moyers, ed. Betty Sue Flowers (New York: Doubleday, 1988) 22.

[8]Barbara C. Sproul, Primal Myths, Creating the World (San Francisco: Harper & Row, 1979) 11.

[9]Jacques Waardenburg, "Symbolic Aspects of Myth," Myth, Symbol, and Reality, ed. Alan M. Olson, vol. 1 of the Boston University Studies in Philosophy and Religion, ed. Leroy S. Rouner (Notre Dame, Indiana: University of Notre Dame Press, 1980) 64.

[10]Alan W. Watts, "Foreword," Charles H. Long, Alpha: The Myths of Creation (Toronto: Collier Books, 1969) xi.

[11]Campbell 55.

[12]John Pemberton, "Eshu-Elegba: The Yoruba Trickster God," African Arts October 1976: 66.

[13]Philip Freund, Myths of Creation (Levittown, New Jersey: Transatlantic Arts, 1975) 233.

[14]Gregory Bateson, Steps to an Ecology of Mind; quoted in Bob Samples, The Metaphoric Mind: A Celebration of Creative Consciousness (Reading, Massachusetts: Addison-Wesley Publishing Co., Inc., 1976) ix.

[15]Ladislas Segy, Masks of Black Africa (New York: Dover Publications, 1976) 8.

[16]Sproul 16.

[17]Kees W. Bolle, The Freedom of Man in Myth (Nashville: Vanderbilt University Press, 1968) 5.

[18]William G. Doty, Mythography: The Study of Myths and Rituals (University: The University of Alabama Press, 1986) 4.

[19]Dorothy Jean Ray, Eskimo Masks: Art and Ceremony (Seattle: University of Washington Press, 1975) 10.

[20]Eliade 13.

[21]Mircea Eliade, "The Sacred and the Modern Artist," Symbolism, the Sacred, and the Arts, ed. Diane Apostolos-Cappadona (New York: Crossroad, 1988) 83.

[22]Joseph Campbell, The Inner Reaches of Outer Space: Metaphor as Myth and as Religion (New York: Alfred van der Marck Editions, 1986) 19.

[23]Marie-Louise von Franz, Patterns of Creativity Mirrored in Creation Myths (Zürich: Spring Publications, 1978) 11.

[24]Waardenburg 54.

[25]Ernst Cassirer, Language and Myth, trans. Suzanne K. Langer (New York: Dover Publications, 1946) 98.

[26]Elizabeth Abel, "Redefining the Sister Arts: Baudelaire's Response to the Art of Delacroix," The Language of Images, ed. W. J. T. Mitchell (Chicago: University of Chicago Press, 1980) 41.

[27]metonymic: using the name of one thing for that of another of which it is an attribute or with which it is associated.

[28]Ernest B. Gilman, "Word and Image in Quarles' Emblemes," The Language of Images, ed. W. J. T. Mitchell (Chicago: University of Chicago Press, 1980) 63.

[29]Joseph Campbell, Myths to Live By (New York: The Viking Press, 1972) 31; specific illustrations of various metaphoric images and an explicit discussion of the ability of metaphor to transcend the mundane and profane by creatively expressing insights into the basic phenomena of life will be developed in the body of this paper; see outline on pages i-ii.

[30]Ian G. Barbour, Myths, Models and Paradigms: A Comparative Study in Science and Religion (New York: Harper & Row, 1976) 13.

[31]Segy 10.

[32]Waardenburg 43-44.

[33]Eliade, Images 178.

[34]Martin Foss, Symbol and Metaphor in Human Experience (Lincoln: University of Nebraska Press, 1949) 146.

[35]Mircea Eliade, "The Symbolism of Shadows in Archaic Religions," Symbolism, the Sacred, and the Arts, ed. Diane Apostolos-Cappadona (New York: Crossroad, 1988) 13.

[36]Foss 111; see also Máscaras 15: "en muchas ocasiones la elaboracion de la mascara es parte del ritual y requiere que el individual este en un estado de pureza fisica y espiritual."

[37]Foss 120.

[38]Eliade, Images 173.

[39]David Attenborough, The Tribal Eye (London: British Broadcasting Corporation, 1976) 140.

[40]Paul Veyne, Did the Greeks Believe in their Myths? An Essay on the Constitutive Imagination, trans. Paula Wissing (Chicago: The University of Chicago Press, 1988) 110.

[41]Doty 117.

[42]Eliade, _Images_ 12.

[43]Foss 110.

[44]Bolle xiii.

[45]Wingert 72.

[46]W. J. T. Mitchell, "Spatial Form in Literature: Toward a General Theory," _The Language of Images_, ed. W. J. T. Mitchell (Chicago: University of Chicago Press, 1980) 298-299.

[47]Campbell, _Inner_ 18.

BIBLIOGRAPHY

Abel, Elizabeth. "Redefining the Sister Arts: Baude-
    laire's Response to the Art of Delacroix." The
    Language of Images. Ed. W. J. T. Mitchell. Chicago:
    The University of Chicago Press, 1980. 37-58.

Attenborough, David. The Tribal Eye. London: British
    Broadcasting Corporation, 1976.

Barbour, Ian G. Myths, Models and Paradigms: A Compar-
    ative Study in Science and Religion. New York:
    Harper & Row, 1976.

Bolle, Kees W. The Freedom of Man in Myth. Nashville:
    Vanderbilt University Press, 1968.

Campbell, Joseph. The Inner Reaches of Outer Space:
    Metaphor as Myth and as Religion. New York:
    Alfred van der Marck Editions, 1986.

---. Myths to Live By. New York: The Viking Press,
    1972.

---. The Power of Myth with Bill Moyers. Ed. Betty
    Sue Flowers. New York: Doubleday, 1988.

Cassirer, Ernst. Language and Myth. Trans. Susanne K.
    Langer. New York: Dover Publications, 1946.

Doty, William G. Mythography: The Study of Myths and
    Rituals. University: The University of Alabama
    Press, 1986.

Eliade, Mircea. Images and Symbols. Trans. Philip
    Mairet. Kansas City, Missouri: Sheed Andrews and
    McMeel, 1961.

---. "The Sacred and the Modern Artist." Symbolism,
    the Sacred, and the Arts. Ed. Diane Apostolos-Cap-
    padona. New York: Crossroad, 1988. 81-85.

---. "The Symbolism of Shadows in Archaic Religions."
    Symbolism, the Sacred, and the Arts. Ed. Diane
    Apostolos-Cappadona. New York: Crossroad, 1988.
    3-16.

Foss, Martin. Symbol and Metaphor in Human
    Experience. Lincoln: University of Nebraska Press,
    1949.

Freund, Philip. Myths of Creation. Levittown, New
   Jersey: Transatlantic Arts, 1975.

Genesis. The Bible. Revised Standard Version.

Gilman, Ernest B. "Word and Image in Quarles'
   Emblemes." The Language of Images. Ed. W. J. T.
   Mitchell. Chicago: The University of Chicago
   Press, 1980. 59-84.

Gingerich, Willard. "Heidegger and the Aztecs: The
   Poetics of Knowing in Pre-Hispanic Nahuatl
   Poetry." Recovering the Word: Essays on Native
   American Literature. Ed. Brian Swann and Arnold
   Krupat. Berkeley: University of California Press,
   1987. 85-112.

Highwater, Jamake. The Primal Mind: Vision and Reality in Indian America. New York: Harper & Row,
   1981.

---. Máscaras Mexicanas: de la Colleción del Ing.
   Victor José Moya. México: Dirección de Museos del
   Instituto Nacional de Antropología e Historia,
   1974.

Mitchell, W. J. T. "Spatial Form in Literature:
   Toward a General Theory." The Language of Images.
   Ed. W. J. T. Mitchell. Chicago: The University of
   Chicago Press, 1980. 271-299.

Pemberton, John. "Eshu-Elegba: The Yoruba Trickster
   God." African Arts October 1975: 20-27, 66-70, 90-92.

Ray, Dorothy Jean. Eskimo Masks: Art and Ceremony.
   Seattle: University of Washington Press, 1975.

Samples, Bob. The Metaphoric Mind: A Celebration of
   Creative Consciousness. Reading, Massachusetts:
   Addison-Wesley Publishing Company, Inc., 1976.

Segy, Ladislas. Masks of Black Africa. New York:
   Dover Publications, 1976.

Sproul, Barbara C. Primal Myths: Creating the World.
   San Francisco: Harper & Row, 1979.

Taylor, Joshua C. "Two Visual Excursions." The Language of Images. Ed. W. J. T. Mitchell. Chicago:
   The University of Chicago Press, 1980. 25-36.

Veyne, Paul. <u>Did</u> <u>the</u> <u>Greeks</u> <u>Believe</u> <u>in</u> <u>their</u> <u>Myths</u>? <u>An</u> <u>Essay</u> <u>on</u> <u>the</u> <u>Constitutive</u> <u>Imagination</u>. Trans. Paula Wissing. Chicago: The University of Chicago Press, 1988.

von Franz, Marie-Louise. <u>Patterns</u> <u>of</u> <u>Creativity</u> <u>Mirrored</u> <u>in</u> <u>Creation</u> <u>Myths</u>. Zürich: Spring Publications, 1978.

Waardenburg, Jacques. "Symbolic Aspects of Myth." <u>Myth</u>, <u>Symbol</u>, <u>and</u> <u>Reality</u>. Ed. Alan M. Olson. Vol. 1 of The Boston University Studies in Philosophy and Religion. Ed. Leroy S. Rouner. Notre Dame, Indiana: University of Notre Dame Press, 1980. 41-68.

Watts, Alan. "Foreword." Charles H. Long. <u>Alpha</u>: <u>The</u> <u>Myths</u> <u>of</u> <u>Creation</u>. Toronto: Collier Book 1969. xi-xii.

Wingert, Paul S. <u>Primitive</u> <u>Art</u>: <u>Its</u> <u>Traditions</u> <u>and</u> <u>Styles</u>. New York: New American Library, 1962.

PLAGIARISM: A STEP TO AVOID*

The only problem of composition that is unique to the research paper is this: you must use and work with the ideas and words of other scholars. Before you are ready for this privilege and its attendant responsibility, you must understand and remember that an idea, though not a tangible article, is just as much the property of another as that person's car or clothes; often it is much more valuable. You must not use it without properly acknowledging your indebtedness. This acknowledgment, far from weakening your paper, will in fact add value and authority to your writing.

If every student understood clearly what plagiarism is, the following illustrations would not be necessary. However, the question of what is honest and what is dishonest use of source material is one that plagues many students; many of the unwary and uninformed have suffered serious consequences academically. As with the entire philosophical question of honesty, there are various degrees of plagiarism. If these examples and your own conscience are inadequate guides, consult the person who is guiding your work on your research paper.

---

*The illustrations for this section are based on the preface reproduced on pages 63–65. It is also reproduced as part of the explanation for the paraphrases (pages 124–127) at the end of this section on plagiarism.

WORD-FOR-WORD PLAGIARISM

I was attracted to mythology because of my fascination with the dramatic action of the stories and the feeling of magic that enters the world in which that action happens. But gradually I realized that on another level those marvelous tales were metaphorical expressions of essential aspects of the human condition. Each social group had obviously developed a body of myths by which it could understand the basic experiences of its existence, such as creation, death, and nature. Although these mythological stories might not be literally true, they do by analogy capture the essential truth both of the basic nature of being and of the society's world view. Von Franz says that when people attempt to explain the unknown, they are likely to depend on imagery from what they do know or on archetypal images which come out of their own inner experiences. Later I realized that these images are also found in primitive art. Mitchell explains that visual representation is not radically distinct from language, and Elizabeth Abel claims that the underlying concepts of myth and art are similar in that both express a common inner source in which the subject matter changes but the nature is the same. I was challenged to investigate the common denominators of the verbal and visual expressions of these insights and to do a comparative study of their metaphoric forms.

COMMENT: Transposing or substituting a few words will not create a paraphrase. In this example, after saying "I was attracted to" instead of "My earliest attraction," the writer of this nearly verbatim piece of plagiarism simply used different words or reworded some short phrases: "was based on" was changed to "because of my"; "narratives" became "stories"; "pervades" became "enters"; "aura" became "feeling"; "takes place" became "happens"; "mythology" became "body of myths," etc. In two other instances the order of the words was reversed: "creation, nature, and death" became "creation, death, and nature" and the order of "basic nature of being" was reversed with "society's world view." Both the paraphrased passage and the directly quoted passages so carefully documented in the original were used here without any documentation. As written, this passage is almost purely a word-for-word copy of the source, retaining even the sentence structure and organization of the original. Even the use of a footnote could not save this paragraph from being condemned.

PATCHWORK PLAGIARISM

I was attracted to <u>mythology</u> because of my childhood <u>fascination with the dramatic action of the</u> magic-like stories they contain. Now, in college <u>I realize that</u> there is <u>another level</u> to the <u>marvelous tales;</u> they are <u>metaphorical expressions of essential aspects of the human condition.</u> All cultures seem to have <u>a mythology</u> that helps them <u>understand the basic experiences of</u> their <u>existence.</u> Even though many of these myths could never be scientifically proved, they do seem to parallel the meaning of a society's belief. **<u>When people attempt to explain the unknown, they</u> use <u>archetypal images which come out of inner experiences.</u> *<u>I realized</u> too <u>that</u> some of these <u>images</u> can be <u>found in primitive art</u> which <u>is not radically distinct from language</u> which shows <u>that the underlying concepts of myth and art are similar</u> because they <u>both express</u> the same <u>subject matter</u> which <u>changes but whose nature</u> is the same. My paper will <u>investigate the common denominators of the verbal and visual expressions of these</u> ideas <u>and</u> I will compare <u>their metaphoric forms.</u>

COMMENT: Changing a single word in a passage otherwise quoted verbatim does not produce a paraphrase. The starred passage (**) would still need to be in quotation marks and footnoted; the changes you make within a quoted passage should go in square brackets, as do all editorial changes and additions; ellipsis marks are used to indicate omissions from the source being quoted. Thus the starred (*) sentence above should be: I realized too that some of these images can be "found in primitive art…[which] is not radically distinct from language" according to Mitchell which shows, Elizabeth Abel says "that the underlying concepts of myth and art are similar." The footnote number would then follow the quotation marks.

When whole phrases are lifted out and are put into a framework of your own wording or into a "different" arrangement of the original, the result is also called plagiarism. In the example given, the underlined phrases are lifted verbatim from the original. Though you would never be expected to put quotation marks merely around such phrases as "I realized," "when people attempt to explain," or "inner experiences," since they are part of our common idiom, you could not write such a sentence as the one marked ** and call it your own. This "rearrangement" is not really a paraphrasing. The sentence preceding it might be called a paraphrase but would still need a footnote; it is very awkwardly stated because the implications of the idea expressed were obviously not very clear to the writer. If all the underlined phrases were in quotation marks, the paragraph would resemble an old-fashioned patchwork quilt. It would also be quite unreadable and certainly not original. Not only is Markman not given credit for her work in the plagiarized version, but the sources *she* carefully documented have also been plagiarized.

"LIFTING OUT THE PERFECT PHRASES"

The aura of magic that pervades mythology and my early fascination with the dramatic action of the stories stimulated my interest in myths. That they were metaphorical expressions explaining creation, nature, and death was clear to me as I became more sophisticated. As metaphors they could by analogy capture the essential truth that was close to each social group so that it could understand the basic experiences of its existence. The imagery, when people attempt to explain the unknown comes from their own worldly experiences or from archetypal images that are part of their inner psyches as we find from illustrations found on maps of antiquity. Since art is not radically distinct from language,[1] I would like to investigate the common denominators of the insights of primitive people as they expressed them verbally in their myths and visually in their art to see if the nature is the same and to study the metaphoric forms of each of them.

---

[1] W. J. T. Mitchell, "Spatial Form in Literature: Towards a General Theory," The Language of Images, ed. W. J. T. Mitchell (Chicago: The University of Chicago Press, 1980) 296.

COMMENT: Though more subtle and clever, this kind of plagiarism is similar to the preceding patchwork illustration. The "perfect phrases" irresistible to the writer here are underlined so you may spot them easily. However, the order in which they appear is often altered.

The words that are underlined with wavy lines might be called paraphrases but could not be used without footnotes. The phrasing "the insights of primitive people as they expressed them verbally in their myths and visually in their art" certainly reflects Markman's idea and, though paraphrased, must be documented as having been quoted from Markman.

Two other serious errors were made in this paragraph:

1. Mitchell was cited in a footnote as if his article were a source used by the writer. (If you did not read the article, you may not cite it.)

2. Not content with "lifting" material from the Preface, the writer has copied the words "found on maps of antiquity" from Marie-Louise von Franz so carefully quoted in Markman's footnotes.

PARAPHRASE

PREFACE

My earliest attraction to mythology was based on a fascination with the

Myths fascinate on several levels. They are

dramatic action of the narratives and the aura of magic that pervades the

imaginative stories that have magic appeal.

world in which that action takes place. But gradually I realized that on

Moreover, the sophisticated scholar can see that

another level those marvelous tales were metaphorical expressions of

by their imagery they are able to capture the essence

essential aspects of the human condition. Each social group had obviously

of some of humanity's most important experiences,

developed a mythology by which it could understand the basic experiences

including how people came into being, their

of its existence, such as creation, nature, and death. Although their

relationship to the world around them, and death.

mythological stories might not be literally true, they do by analogy capture

Apparently every society develops a body of myths in order

the essential truth both of the society's world view and of the basic nature of

to understand these basic mysteries of life. Even though

being. Von Franz says that when people attempt to explain the unknown,

there is no way to prove anything scientifically, the central

they are likely to depend on imagery from what they do know or on

metaphors of the stories do express the essence of

archetypal images which come out of their own inner experiences.[1]

truth about the human condition. In her book about

Later I realized that these images are also found in primitive art. Mitchell

creation myths, for example, Marie Louise von Franz

explains that visual representation is "not radically distinct from language,"[2]

says that the metaphors are based on imagery either

and Elizabeth Abel contends that the underlying concepts of myth and art

from people's own experiences or from the primordial images of their psyches, ①and both W.J.T. Mitchell and Elizabeth Abel suggest that the same imagery

are similar in that both express a "common inner source whose subject

is often found in art forms even though the actual

matter changes but whose nature is the same."[3] I was challenged to

subject may not be the same. ②A comparison of the

investigate the common denominators of the verbal and visual expressions

two forms of expression would result in a very

of these insights and to do a comparative study of their metaphoric forms.

valuable study to discover the "truths" expressed in the metaphoric imagery that primitive societies have left us in their art and in their mythology.

[1]Marie-Louise von Franz, *Patterns of Creativity Mirrored in Creation Myths* (Zürich, Spring Publications, 1978) 5. Von Franz bases her conclusions on the images she has found on maps of antiquity.

[2]W. J. T. Mitchell, "Spatial Form in Literature: Toward a General Theory," *The Language of Images*, ed. W. J. T. Mitchell (Chicago: The University of Chicago Press, 1980) 296. Mitchell reinforces his point with a quote from Ludwig Wittgenstein's *Philosophical Investigations*: "A picture held us captive. And we could not get outside it, for it lay in our language and language seemed to repeat it to us inexorably" (Mitchell 271).

[3]Elizabeth Abel, "Redefining the Sister Arts: Baudelaire's Response to the Art of Delacroix," *The Language of Images*, ed. W. J. T. Mitchell (Chicago: The University of Chicago Press, 1980) 41.

> [1] Marie-Louise von Franz, *Patterns of Creativity Mirrored in Creation Myths* (Zürich: Spring Publications, 1978), 5; quoted in Roberta H. Markman, "The Metaphoric Vision in Mythology and Art," master's thesis, California State University Long Beach, 1982, iv.
>
> [2] W. J. T. Mitchell, "Spatial Form in Literature: Toward a General Theory" and Elizabeth Abel, "Redefining the Sister Arts: Baudelaire's Response to the Art of Delacroix," both in *The Language of Images*, ed. W. J. T. Mitchell (Chicago: The University of Chicago Press, 1980), 41, 271; quoted in Roberta H. Markman, "The Metaphoric Vision in Mythology and Art," master's thesis, California State University, Long Beach, 1982, iv.

COMMENT: This is a paraphrase, for the writer here has followed the source, sentence by sentence and idea by idea but has used his or her own words. There is value in doing this (see the reasons listed preceding card F on pp. 60–61), but remember that you must not alter the sense of the original.

Also remember: although the words in a paraphrase (or a précis) may be truly your own, the thoughts and opinions are not; therefore you must acknowledge your indebtedness to the thinking of the original writer by giving your source in a parenthetical reference or footnote. (*See* STEP 9.)

REMEMBER: Of the four preceding examples, only the paraphrase could be used without quotation marks, and even it would require documentation. THE OTHER EXAMPLES WOULD BE CALLED PLAGIARISM *EVEN WITH* DOCUMENTATION.

THE LIBRARY: A STEP TO MASTER

USING THE LIBRARY FOR BOOKS AND OTHER COMMUNICATIONS MEDIA

The library is the most valuable storehouse of information on almost every subject for anyone doing research. It is essential, therefore, to become familiar with the tools in your library and to make use of as many of them as your time affords.

1. The Online Computer Catalog and/or The Card Catalog

All students should consider the online computer catalog and/or the card catalog as their most valuable index. When you locate an entry for a book you want, it is essential to copy the entire call number accurately, since it is the most important mark of identification for locating any book.

2. Computer Searches

Online library searches enable students to conduct their own self-service bibliographic computer search of the indexes and abstracts that exist in a particular area of study. Depending on the database you use, you can search for a bibliographic list or a full text of the articles. This is the fastest means of establishing your preliminary bibliography. (*See* STEP 4, pp. 16–20.)

3. The Reference Rooms

Become familiar with the basic reference texts in your particular subject. The periodical indexes, special indexes, bibliographies, and special encyclopedias (see pages 138–143) are in the reference room of the library. Ask at the information desk to find out whether or not the library has reference rooms for different subjects or whether all references may be found in one place.

4. Special Sections

In larger libraries there are often special rooms for collections of bibliographies, circulating art prints and slides, periodicals, audiovisual aids, photograph records, tapes, pamphlets, rare books and folios, newspapers, reserve books, dissertations and other unpublished manuscripts, maps, and other special materials, each of which may have its own separate catalog or listing; hence it is important for you to check these various sections in your particular library as you search for relevant materials.

5. Films, Filmstrips, and Videotapes

Many libraries afford students the opportunity to view films, filmstrips, and videotapes; often, arrangements must be made in advance for this privilege.

6. Pamphlets

Pamphlets are a valuable source of additional current information on any subject. Often they are circulated, although they will not be found listed in the card catalog. Even a little pamphlet can contain great ideas.

7. Microfilms and Microfiche

Microfilms and microfiche have enabled libraries to store and mail copies of books that would not otherwise be available. Microfilm reading machines are easy to use and very interesting; you may even find that the machine helps you to keep awake between pages. Microfiche require the use of a microprint reading machine which is also simple to handle; it enables a library to have an entire work on a single card. In a busy library, be sure to make arrangements in advance for the use of these miraculous machines.

8. Records, Compact Discs, and Audiotapes

Although many students may not be aware of it, music is not the only material that is available on phonograph records and tapes. You should check these for recordings of lectures and readings on every subject, since some of these may not be available in other media.

9. Newspapers

All issues of the most important newspapers are available on microfilm; they are often listed in the holding file of a periodical room.

10. Periodicals

Many periodical indexes are available in the reference room of the library. (*See* pages 138–143.) After you have found the source of an article that interests you, check the holding file of periodicals to find out if the periodical you need is available in your library. Issues of periodicals published in the same year have the same volume number and are eventually bound together in the same volume; so if you need several issues with the same volume number (of a bound periodical), you need to ask or look for only one bound volume. Often you can arrange to borrow those that are not available in your library, but this entails using the interlibrary loan service discussed under 13d following.

11. Picture File

Mounted magazine pictures, commercially prepared study prints, and pictorial maps are often available through the library. These can be valuable aids in many areas of research. Art prints are often available on loan for you to enjoy at home or in your own room for a considerable length of time.

12. Stack Privileges

Depending on the regulations of each individual library, some students have the privilege of going directly to the library stacks, a privilege that will enable them to look at all the works in sections (or call numbers) related to their research subjects. If you have this privilege, this chance to browse will reveal material that you might not have found in the card catalog. It is important to use the indexes of the various books that seem relevant in order to ascertain their value to your project.

13. Special Services

Your library is often equipped to offer you many special services:

a. Renewal of books you have not finished using.

b. "Holding" a book that someone else has taken out of the library. If you request a "hold" on a book, your library will notify you when it is returned to the library. It is important to respond quickly to a notice that a "hold" book is waiting for you because your library may have a time limit on this service.

c. Xerox or copying machines are usually available for you to use in copying or duplicating material from a book in the library. Be aware of the copyright laws, however, as only a limited amount of material is legally available for copying.

d. Most libraries subscribe to an interlibrary loan service, which makes available most of the world's materials, even those not in your library. Materials obtained through this service are usually borrowed for a very limited time, so it is wise to find out how long it will take for the material to reach you and how long you may keep it.

There are, of course, many ways in which you will encounter the names of books that you think will be valuable for your research. Usually you will find them in bibliographies by other researchers or referred to in footnotes or appendixes in your sources. Then you should check the *National Union Catalog*, which your librarian will have and with which you can locate books in hundreds of American libraries. Through the interlibrary loan service you can usually obtain the books you need. Winifred Gregory's *Union List of Serials*, though not quite as complete or up to date, also serves the same purpose: it helps you locate periodicals in other libraries. You can find films listed in the *Union List of Microfilms* and *Newspapers on Microfilms*.

e. Typewriters and computers are available for student use in most libraries and are usually coin-operated.

14. The Reference Librarian

The reference librarian is a busy person, but when all else fails he or she is the one who is professionally trained to help you locate materials and use the library to its greatest potential. Solicit the help of a reference librarian only after you have tried to help yourself, but do not hesitate to ask for help when you honestly need it.

APPENDICES

RESEARCH TERMS DEFINED

Research writing, like any other specialized activity, has its own jargon. The following are terms frequently used by people in discussing research:

abridgment: a condensation of the author's original work (expurgated text).

acknowledgment: recognition made of indebtedness to another.

annotated bibliography: a bibliography with comments about each source, telling how inclusive it is, how valuable it is, what the author does and what his or her purpose is, and so on.

authority: a writer whose work and opinions are generally accepted as final and reliable.

autobiography: the writer's own account of his or her life.

bibliography: a list of books, articles, and other material about a single subject, idea, person, and so forth.

biography: a writer's account of the life story of another. There are three types: straight, fictional, and critical.

brackets: the punctuation marks [ ] used only within a quoted passage to enclose additions in your own words (called editorial comment, insertion, or interpolation) explaining a word or giving information needed by the reader.

Brackets may be drawn in black ink if the typewriter has no brackets.

NEVER use unnecessary brackets: "He [Aristotle] wrote an early definition of tragedy"; simply write this: Aristotle "wrote an early definition of tragedy." Parentheses are different and have a different function.

card catalog: a card file listing alphabetically all books in a library.

compile (compilation, compiler): to combine related material. The one who does the combining is a compiler; the result is a compilation.

cross-reference: words or symbols that refer the reader to other places where information about an idea may be found.

Cross-references are used in card catalogs, footnotes, indexes, and bibliographies.

dedication: a page of tribute by the writer to one he or she admires or feels indebted to or wants to honor.

dissertation: a long, involved, and formal exposition on some serious or scholarly subject.

In academic circles, the word is usually reserved for those papers written by a candidate for a doctorate; the word *thesis* indicates the paper written by a candidate for the master's degree.

document: to acknowledge indebtedness for an idea or fact. It is necessary to document the source of any critical opinion (and some facts); *see* STEP 9.

ellipsis: an omission within quoted material indicated by three periods with a space before, after, and between periods (. . .).

The ellipsis marks may indicate the omission of a single word or of whole sentences, but you must never omit words that would change the essential, intended meaning of the quoted material. It is illogical to use an ellipsis to open or to close a quoted passage; hence it would never come immediately after an opening quotation mark nor immediately before the closing quotation mark unless you wish to emphasize the omission of material before or after the passage quoted; it should be used only to show an omission within a quoted passage. Use a fourth period only before a new sentence which begins after an ellipsis within the quoted passage.

endnote: a documentary note placed at the end of a section, chapter, paper, or book rather than at the bottom of the page on which the note number appears.

file: frequently misused as a substitute for the proper term *card catalog*.

The word *file* is properly used to refer to some special library file such as the vertical file, which contains temporarily interesting leaflets, pamphlets, newspaper and magazine clippings, illustrations, and so on that are not permanently classified and filed but are put in standing (vertical) files and removed when the interest fades: as one librarian put it, "temporary stuff and current junk."

footnote: a documentary note placed at the bottom of the page on which the note number appears.

foreword: a note from the author at the front of a book.

Current practice reveals that there is some confusion about the exact distinctions between the sections called *foreword*, *preface*, and *introduction*; however, by whatever name it may be called, this section sets forth an explanation by the author of his or her intended purpose and reason for writing as well as any information or background that might be needed by the reader.

interpolate: to insert an idea or material or information where it should logically go in the organization of the writing.

introduction: a section that follows the table of contents and introduces the work that follows. See *foreword*.

online computer catalog: the computer system used to duplicate or replace the card catalog; see *card catalog*.

pagination: the system for numbering pages of a manuscript or book.

parentheses: the punctuation marks ( ) used to enclose your own explanatory material or words interpolated into a sentence or phrase of your own.

Brackets enclose material more foreign to the context than that put in parentheses; avoid the overuse of either.

parenthetical reference: a documentary note placed within parentheses immediately after the material being documented indicating the source of that material.

plagiarism: a literary word for the thievery of style, ideas, or phrasing.

Plagiarism ranges from the theft of a single word to the deliberate copying (without quotation marks) of a whole passage; it can be avoided by careful note-taking and footnoting (q.v.); everything not documented must be your own original idea and phrasing. You are not writing original sentences of your own if you merely arrange into a new order or sentence pattern some select phrases and sentences taken without quotation marks from your sources. See section entitled "Plagiarism: A Step to Avoid," pages 120–127.

preface: a note from the author which comes before (some put it after) the table of contents or outline.

The preface is frequently followed by a page of acknowledgments; see *foreword*.

primary source: the literature, the work, manuscript, journal, letters, and so on as originally written.

A secondary source is a work written about an original source; a primary source in connection with one subject might be a secondary source in connection with another subject.

For example, a novel by Faulkner would be a primary source for a paper about Faulkner or the novel in America and so on; a Master's thesis on Faulkner would be a primary source for a paper on the writing of theses in American colleges and universities, but it would be a secondary source for a paper on Faulkner.

reference or reference book: any source being read for information. The number and quality of your references will in large measure determine the quality of your finished paper.

rough draft: the first and any subsequent writing before the paper is put in final form.

Rough drafts are subject to drastic and sometimes numerous revisions.

scan: to make a cursory reading of material in order to evaluate it and decide how to read it.

secondary source: a criticism or evaluation of an original piece of writing. See *primary source*.

slug (label, tag): the label on a notecard written above the top line and immediately after the identifying symbol. It may be taken from or may suggest ideas for the outline units.

thesis: the simple statement of opinion which the entire work is designed to support.

See complete explanation and examples in STEP 3.

LIBRARY CLASSIFICATION SYSTEMS

The "call numbers" on the card in the card catalog and on the backs of books usually follow the Library of Congress system or the Dewey decimal system. The former is more often used by college libraries and large collections.

THE LIBRARY OF CONGRESS CLASSIFICATION SYSTEM

The Library of Congress system divides all branches of knowledge into twenty-one main groups which are designated by letters of the alphabet.

Then each branch is further divided by the addition of letters and Arabic numerals, permitting endless combinations. The twenty-one groups are:

A	General Works—Polygraphy
B	Philosophy—Religion
C	History—Auxiliary Sciences
D	History—Topography (except America)
E–F	American History and Topography
G	Geography—Anthropology
H	Social Sciences
J	Political Science
K	Law
L	Education
M	Music
N	Fine Arts
P	Language and Literature
Q	Science
R	Medicine
S	Agriculture—Plant and Animal Husbandry
T	Technology
U	Military Science
V	Naval Science
Z	Bibliography and Library Science

To illustrate the subdivision of an area of knowledge, P designates the Language and Literature category which subdivides:

P	Philology and Linguistics: General
PA	Greek and Latin Philology and Literature
PB	Celtic Language and Literature
PC	Romance Languages (French, Spanish, Italian)
PD	Germanic Languages

THE DEWEY DECIMAL SYSTEM

All branches of knowledge are divided into ten numbered parts according to hundreds, which are then further divided into specific areas of knowledge. The number on the first line is the call number; below it are other lines indicating the code used for author, a particular work, the edition, the number of copies on hand, and so on. The numbers below indicate ways the number on the first line may appear.

000   General Works
100   Philosophy
200   Religion
300   Social Sciences
400   Language (Philology)
500   Pure Science
600   Useful Arts
700   Fine Arts
800   Literature
900   History

These parts are further divided; the second number in the 800's indicates the country or language of the literature.

810   American Literature in English
820   English and Old English
830   Germanic Literature
840   French, Provençal, Catalan
850   Italian, Rumanian
860   Spanish, Portuguese

REFERENCE MATERIALS AND STYLE MANUALS

Most research will start in the reference room of your library; there you will find many volumes written not to be read but to be used as guides to general and to specialized articles and books about all fields of knowledge. These indexes and general reference books are guides only; they do not contain material you will read; they will not be a part of your bibliography. Quite literally, they are tools that you must learn to use, and no amount of explanation will replace experience and an active imagination. Hence the following list contains only the names of a few reference guides and is not annotated. (*See also* "Where to Find a Preliminary Bibliography," pp. 16–25.)

GENERAL WORKS

There are numerous atlases, dictionaries, and encyclopedias that are too familiar to the average student to need listing here.

GUIDES TO REFERENCE SOURCES

Armstrong, C. J., and J. A. Large. *Manual of Online Search Strategies*. Boston: Hall, 1988.

Cuadra Associates. *Directory of Online Databases*. Santa Monica: Cuadra, 1979 to date.

Hillard, James M. *Where to Find What: A Handbook to Reference Service*. Metuchen, New Jersey: Scarecrow Press, 1984.

Mark, Linda, ed. *Reference Sources*, 7 vols. Ann Arbor, Michigan: The Pierian Press, 1983.

Sheehy, Eugene Paul, comp. *Guide to Reference Books*, 10th ed. Chicago: American Library Association, 1986.

Swidan, Eleanor A. *Reference Books, a Brief Guide*, 9th ed. Baltimore: Enoch Pratt Free Library, 1988.

Vitale, Philip H. *Basic Tools of Research*, 3rd ed. Woodbury, New York: Barron's, 1975.

NOTE: These guides give more detailed information about possible sources than you will find in some indexes (such as those that follow).

BIBLIOGRAPHIES AND SUPPLEMENTS TO THE ONLINE COMPUTER CATALOG

Bibliographic Index: A Cumulative Bibliography of Bibliographies. New York: H. W. Wilson, 1934 to date.

The Cumulative Book Index. New York: H. W. Wilson, 1928 to date. (For books in print in English prior to 1928, see *The United States Catalog*, 4th ed. New York: H. W. Wilson, 1928).

Essay and General Literature Index. New York: H. W. Wilson, 1934 to date.

Monthly Catalog of United States Government Publications. Washington, D.C.: Government Printing Office, 1895 to date.

Toomey, Alice F., comp. *A World Bibliography of Bibliographies, 1964–1974*. 2 vols. Totowa, New Jersey: Rowman and Littlefield, 1977.

BIOGRAPHICAL REFERENCE BOOKS AND DICTIONARIES

Biography Index. New York: H. W. Wilson, 1946 to date.
Current Biography. New York: H. W. Wilson, 1940 to date.
Dictionary of American Biography. 22 vols., index, and supplements. New York: Scribner, 1928–1980.
Ethredge, James M., and Barbara Kopala, eds. *Contemporary Authors.* 84 vols. Detroit: Gale Research Corp., 1962 to date.
Thorne, J. O., and T. C. Collocott, eds. *Chambers Biographical Dictionary,* rev. ed. New York: Cambridge UP, 1984.
Webster's Biographical Dictionary. Springfield, Massachusetts: G. & C. Merriam, 1970.
Who's Who. New York: Macmillan, 1849 to date.

REFERENCE BOOKS AND INDEXES ON VARIOUS SUBJECTS

It is almost impossible to draw absolute lines dividing ideas and subjects, to say that one idea concerns just one and no other area of thinking; it is also impossible to define exactly the line distinguishing the subject matter in all the books in a library. The following list therefore makes arbitrary divisions for the sake of convenience. Because reference books are usually kept in the reference room and do not circulate, they are relatively easy to locate without any more information than we have included here.

FINE ARTS AND HUMANITIES

GENERAL: *Humanities Index*
             Union List of Microfilms

ART: *Art Index*
             Art Through the Ages: Gardner
             Encyclopedia of World Art
             *Fine Arts: a Bibliographic Guide to Basic
                Reference Works, Histories, and Handbooks*
             Index to Art Periodicals
             International Dictionary of Art and Artists

McGraw-Hill Dictionary of Art
Oxford Companion to Art

FILM AND DRAMA: *Bibliographic Guide to Theatre Arts*
Complete Film Dictionary
Cumulated Dramatic Index
Dictionary of Films
Film Literature Index
A Guide to Critical Reviews
Index to Plays in Collections
International Encyclopedia of Film
National Union Catalog
Oxford Companion to Film
Play Index

LITERATURE: *American Authors and Books*
Bibliography of American Literature
Bibliography of European Literature
Cambridge Bibliography of English Literature
Cassell's Encyclopedia of World Literature
Granger Index to Poetry
M.L.A. Bibliography

MUSIC: *International Cyclopedia of Music and
Musicians*
Music Index
New Grove Dictionary of Music
Oxford Companion to Music
Schirmer's Guide to Books on Music

PHILOSOPHY: *A Dictionary of Philosophical Concepts*
Dictionary of Philosophy
Encyclopedia of Philosophy
Philosophy Index

THE NATURAL SCIENCES

GENERAL: *Applied Science and Technology Index*
Cambridge Encyclopedia of Astronomy
General Science Index
A Guide to the History of Science
Scientific and Technical Books in Print
Van Nostrand's Scientific Encyclopedia

ASTRONOMY: *Encyclopedia of Astronomy and Astrophysics*
    Larousse Encyclopedia of Astronomy

BIOLOGY: *Encyclopedia of Biological Sciences*
    Biological and Agricultural Index

CHEMISTRY: *Chemical Abstracts*
    Chemical Publications
    How to Find Chemical Information
    Searching the Chemical Literature

GEOGRAPHY: *GEO Abstracts*

PHYSICS: *Encyclopedia of Physics*
    Guide to Literature of Math and Physics
    Physics Abstracts

THE SOCIAL SCIENCES

GENERAL: *A Reader's Guide to the Social Sciences*
    International Encyclopedia of the Social Sciences
    Social Science Index
    The Social Sciences: A Cross-Disciplinary Guide to Selected Resources

ANTHROPOLOGY: *Abstracts in Anthropology*

BUSINESS: *Business Periodicals Index*
    Encyclopedia of Economics
    Sources of Business Information

POLITICAL SCIENCE: *International Political Science Abstracts*
    The Literature of Political Science

PSYCHOLOGY: *Dictionary of Philosophy and Psychology*
    Dictionary of Psychology
    Encyclopedia of Psychology
    List of Books in Psychology

RELIGION: *Encyclopedia of Religion and Ethics*
    International Standard Bible Encyclopedia

SOCIOLOGY: *Sociological Abstracts*

SCIENCE AND TECHNOLOGY

GENERAL:
Applied Science & Technology Index
Harper Encyclopedia of Science
McGraw Hill Encyclopedia of Science and Technology
Scientific and Technical Books in Print

COMPUTER
SCIENCE:
Computer and Control Abstracts

ENERGY:
Energy Index

ENGINEERING:
Engineering Index
Sources of Engineering Information

ENVIRONMENTAL
SCIENCES:
Pollution Abstracts

NURSING:
Cumulative Index to Nursing Literature

STYLE MANUALS

Every discipline has its preferred style for the preparation and documentation of scholarly writing. Although most instructors would suggest that you use the formats outlined for you in this book, if you are doing advanced research, you might want to consult the guide used in your field of study, for example:

BIOLOGY

Council of Biology Editors, Style Manual Committee. *CBE Style Manual: A Guide for Authors, Editors, and Publishers in the Biological Sciences.* 6th ed. Bethesda, Maryland: Council of Biology Editors, 1992.

BUSINESS AND ECONOMICS

Dawe, Jessamon. *Writing Business and Economics Papers, Theses and Dissertations.* Totowa, New Jersey: Littlefield, Adams, 1975.

CHEMISTRY

Dodd, Janet S. *The ACS Style Guide: A Manual for Authors and Editors*. Washington, D.C.: American Chemical Society, 1986.

ENGINEERING

American Institute of Chemical Engineers. *Guide for Writers and Speakers*. New York: American Institute of Chemical Engineers, n.d.

Institute of Electrical and Electronic Engineers. "Information for IEEE Authors." *IEEE Spectrum* August 1965: 11–15.

Society of Mining Engineers. *Author's Guide*. Littleton, Colorado: Society of Mining Engineers-AIME, 1983.

GEOPHYSICAL SCIENCES

Cochran, Wendell, Peter Fenner, and Mary Hill, eds. *Geowriting: A Guide to Writing, Editing, and Printing in Earth Science*. Alexandria, Virginia: American Geological Institute, 1984.

United States Geological Survey. *Suggestions to Authors of the Reports of the United States Geological Survey*. 6th ed. Washington, D.C.: Government Printing Office, 1978.

GOVERNMENT

Garner, Diane L., and Diane H. Smith. *The Complete Guide to Citing Government Documents: A Manual for Writers and Librarians*. Bethesda, Maryland: Congressional Information Service, 1984.

Rodgers, Frank. *A Guide to British Government Documents*. New York: H. W. Wilson Company, 1980.

A Uniform System of Citation, 14th ed. Cambridge, Massachusetts: Harvard Law Review Association, 1986.

United States Government Printing Office. *Style Manual*. Rev. ed. Washington, D.C.: Government Printing Office, 1984.

HUMANITIES

Gibaldi, Joseph, and Walter S. Achtert. *MLA Handbook for Writers of Research Papers*. 3rd ed. New York: The Modern Language Association of America, 1988.

LINGUISTICS

Linguistic Society of America. Appears in each December issue of the *LSA Bulletin*.

MATHEMATICS

American Mathematical Society. *A Manual for Authors of Mathematical Papers*. 9th ed. Providence, Rhode Island: American Mathematical Soceity, 1990.

MEDICINE

Barclay, William R. *Manual for Authors and Editors: Editoral Style and Manuscript Preparation*. 7th ed. Los Altos, California: Lange Medical Publications, 1981.

International Steering Committee of Medical Editors. "Uniform Requirements for Manuscripts Submitted to Biomedical Journals." *Annals of Internal Medicine* January 1979: 95–99.

MUSIC

Irvine, Demar, ed. *Writing about Music: A Style Book for Reports and Theses*. 2nd ed. Seattle: University of Washington Press, 1968.

PHYSICS

Publication Board, American Institute of Physics, *Style Manual for Guidance in the Preparation of Papers*. 4th ed. New York: American Institute of Physics, 1990.

PSYCHOLOGY
(widely used in the other social sciences)

American Psychological Association. *Publication Manual of the American Psychological Association*. 3rd ed. Washington, D.C.: American Psychological Association, 1983.

GENERAL

The following guides are used in a wide variety of fields. (The *MLA Handbook for Writers of Research Papers* and the *Publication Manual of the American Psychological Association* previously listed might also be considered general guides because of their wide acceptance outside their own disciplines.)

The Chicago Manual of Style, 14th ed. Chicago: The University of Chicago Press, 1993.

Turabian, Kate L. *A Manual for Writers of Term Papers, Theses, and Dissertations*. 5th ed. Chicago: The University of Chicago Press, 1987.

ABBREVIATIONS USED IN RESEARCH

anon.	anonymous
bk., bks.	book(s)
c., ca.	*circa*: "about"; for approximate dates (c. 1884, ca. 1884)
cf.	*confer*: "compare"; not a synonym for *see*
chap., ch., chs.	chapter(s)
col., cols.	column(s)
comp.	compiler, compiled, compiled by
ed., eds.	editor(s), edition(s), or edited by
e.g.	*exempli gratia*: "for example"
et al.	*et alii*: "and others"
et seq.	*et sequens*: "and the following" (or ff., which is shorter)
ex.	example
f., ff.	and the following page(s) (pp. 79f. or pp.79ff)
fig., figs.	figure(s)
ibid.	*ibidem*: "in the same place as quoted above"; refers to title in footnote immediately above;

	author's name not given; page given if different from the one preceding
i.e.	*id est*: "that is"; preceded by a comma and followed by a comma and list or explanation
ill., illus.	illustration; illustrated by
l., ll.	line(s)
loc. cit.	*loco citato*: "in the place cited"; refers to work fully identified in any previous footnote except the one immediately preceding; preceded by author's last name; never followed by a page number because *loc. cit.* means "in the same location" (page) as in last footnote referring to that source
MS (MSS)	manuscript(s); always capitalized; no period
N.B.	*nota bene*: "take notice; mark well"; always capitalized
n.d.	no date given
no., nos.	number(s)
n.p.	no place of publication (and/or no publisher) given
op. cit.	*opere citato*: "in the work cited"; preceded by author's last name and followed by page number (because *op. cit.* stands for title only); refers to work cited previously but not immediately above
p., pp.	page(s)
passim	"throughout the work, here and there"; (p. 37 et passim means p. 37 and other scattered pages; or pp. 37–42 passim)
pl., pls.	plate(s)
pseud.	pseudonym, pen name (Lewis Carroll, Mark Twain)
pt.	part
q.v.	*quod vide*: "which see"
rev.	reviewed by; revised or revised by; revision
rpt.	reprint
sc.	scene
sec. secs.	section(s)
sic	"thus"; not an abbreviation; used within brackets to indicate that an error in quote is in the original: "It was to [sic] bad."
st.	stanza
tr., trans.	translator, translation, translated by
v., vv.	verse(s)

viz.   *videlicet*: "namely"; use with or without a period; usage varies

vol., vols.   volume(s); capitalize only before Roman numeral: Vol. VII; 9 vols.

ROMAN NUMERALS

I	V	X	L	C	D	M
1	5	10	50	100	500	1000

To read a number with two or more Roman numerals, start with the larger numeral and subtract what is to the left; add what is to the right.

If a numeral is between two of greater value, subtract it from the second and then add that number (the remainder) to the first:

$$MCMLXXI = 1971$$

A bar over a numeral multiplies it by 1000. Roman numerals may be written in capitals or in lower case.

$$IX = 9 \quad XXXII = 32 \quad XL = 40 \quad CL = 150$$
$$CD = 400 \quad CDV = 405$$
$$DC = 600 \quad CM = 900 \quad \overline{IV} = 4000$$

Use Roman numerals in capitals (IV, XII, CDL) when you want

to indicate volumes of books in series;
to number the acts in a play;
to number the books (or the cantos) of a long poem;
to identify different people with the same name (George III);
to indicate major divisions in an outline.

Use Roman numerals in lowercase (ii, iv, xii) when you want

to number all prefatory pages including outline and table of contents;
to identify scenes in a drama.

BASIC PUNCTUATION

Punctuating your research paper will be easy if you learn these basic rules that apply to the structures or patterns most frequently used in writing. If you keep the following rules in mind, especially those pertaining to the use of the comma, your paper will be clear and effective.

1. The Apostrophe

a. Use an apostrophe with an *s* to show possession (belonging to): Mary's hat, the heart's desire. *Except*, if the word ends in *s*, then add the apostrophe after the *s*: the Smiths' book (belonging to the Smith family). On occasion, for the sake of pronunciation, a word ending in *s* forms the possessive by adding *es*: The Williamses book (belonging to the Williams family).

b. Use an apostrophe to show that a letter has been omitted: it's/it is; who's/who is; there's/there is.

NOTE: Possessive pronouns have their own forms and do not require an apostrophe: mine, yours, his, their(s), its.

2. The Comma

Do not use a comma unless one of the following rules apply:

a. Use a comma before a coordinating conjunction (or, and, but, for, yet, nor, etc.) in a compound sentence: I did my work, but I forgot to hand it in.

b. Use a comma between items (nouns, clauses, phrases, etc.) in a series of three or more, except before the last item when a conjunction is used: I bought apples, oranges, peaches, and bananas.

c. Use a comma between adjectives preceding a noun: This is a quiet, peaceful hotel. *Except*, if you cannot substitute *and* for the comma, do not use the comma: I have a small black cat.

d. Use a comma after an introductory modifier: Yes, I did it. Well, I'm going now.

e. Use a comma after an introductory prepositional phrase *only* if the phrase is long: In order to succeed in college and prepare for the future, one must study.

f. Use a comma to prevent misreading: Once inside, the dog began to bark.

g. Use commas to set off an appositive (an expression following a noun which means the same thing and can be used in place of the noun): Larry Jones, the student standing by the door, scored highest on the exam.

h. Use commas to set off a parenthetical statement (an expression inserted to explain or emphasize): Mary, for example, never studied. John, on the other hand, always did.

i. Use commas to set off a direct address: His comments, my dear friend, cannot be repeated.

j. Use commas to set off an expression inserted into a direct quotation: "Now," he said, "the class is dismissed."

k. Use a comma to show contrast: This is a college, not a university. She is a freshman, not a senior.

l. Use commas to set off a nonrestrictive clause or phrase (an expression that is not necessary for understanding, but does provide additional information): My mother, who is a teacher, came to see me.

m. Use commas to set off an absolute phrase (an expression consisting of a noun or pronoun and a participle that modifies the sentence as a whole): Weather permitting, we can study together tonight.

n. Use a comma before *such as* when it is used to introduce an example: She is interested in many occult subjects, such as magic, astrology, and mind reading.

3. The Semicolon

a. Use a semicolon to separate two independent clauses not joined by a conjunction: I went to see him; he was not there.

b. Use a semicolon between equal elements that contain commas: John, president; Paula, vice-president; Jane, treasurer; and so on.

4. The Colon

Use a colon after a complete statement to draw attention to what follows: She had many hobbies: painting, swimming, tennis, and reading.

5. Quotation Marks

a. Use quotation marks before and after words that are exactly copied: "Well," Mary said, "this is a happy day." Note the position of the quotation marks *after* the comma and the period.

b. Use quotation marks to identify titles of essays, individual poems, songs, stories, which are part of larger works.

6. The Hyphen

Use a hyphen between words used as a single modifier before a noun: He is a well-known writer. This is a half-finished job.

7. Underlining

Underline titles of books, magazines, and other complete works.

In addition to these basic rules, see the index for particular marks of punctuation discussed in various sections of this book.

INDEX